IRON DUKE PUI

# THE WISDOM OF LEADERS

History's Most Powerful
Leadership Quotes, Ideas, and Advice

## Volume I
of The Leadership Development Series

## DEREK WELLINGTON JOHNSON

Iron Duke Publishing

© Derek Wellington Johnson 2018

ISBN 978-1-7335489-0-8

# Dedication

To my father, you were the first leader to teach me about life, honor, discipline, integrity and more. I wish you had lived longer. I had so many more questions to ask you.

# CONTENTS

# Part Three
# Mastering a Leadership Mindset

# Biographies

"History is the record of man's steps and slips. It shows us that the steps have been slow and slight; the slips, quick and abounding. It provides us with the opportunity to profit by the stumbles and tumbles of our forerunners."

– Bevin Alexander

"Where are our men of abilities? Why do they not come forth to save their country?"

– George Washington

"Since it has been my intention to write something which may be of use to the understanding reader, it has seemed wiser to me to follow the real truth of the matter rather than what we imagine it to be. For imagination has created many principalities and republics that have never been seen or known to have any real existence, for how we live is so different from how we ought to live that he who studies what ought to be done rather than what is done will learn the way to his downfall rather than to his preservation."

– Niccolò Machiavelli, *The Prince*

# Introduction

My father served as a tank commander in legendary General George S. Patton's 3rd Army. He saw fierce fighting and had the scars on his body as a constant reminder of his time in World War II. When I was born many years later, my father's time in combat was still an integral part of who he was. It was as if the war had permanently fused itself onto his soul. By the time I was eleven years old, I not only knew who Patton was, but also the intense level of respect that my father had for him. My father spoke to me of leaders such as Hannibal, Alexander the Great, Genghis Khan, Napoleon, Julius Caesar, Marcus Aurelius, and The Duke of Wellington who would end up defeating Napoleon at the Battle of Waterloo.

My father told me stories about history's greatest leaders. Through those stories and by my father's example, I learned about honor, integrity, perseverance, courage, teamwork and of course, leadership.

My father died when I was 16. The WWII war veteran fought a tenacious battle against lung cancer, and had lived well past the point when he should have died. I remember being at the hospital one day overhearing my father's doctor telling my mother that based on the amount of lung tissue he had left, there was no way that he should still be alive, and yet he was. Less than a week later my father went to Valhalla, the place where valiant Viking warriors went after they had been slain.

Losing him put my life into a tailspin. With no other strong male influences in my life, I floundered. Somehow I found myself in my high school library later that year, and while mindlessly perusing old dusty books I came across one that called out to me. It was Meditations by the great Caesar Marcus Aurelius. My father had mentioned it to me when I was a boy, but I had not given it any thought since then.

I took the old book with me to an isolated corner of the library and started reading. I felt like a parched desert that had finally been hydrated with much needed rain. And so began my love affair; my obsession with great leaders. They became my surrogate father. They mentored me and gave me guidance during periods of my life when I was lost and didn't know which way to turn. They were my guideposts when I was in the military, through my bitter divorce, my journeys in the startup world, and all the other times when I needed someone to help illuminate a path out of the darkness.

I shudder to think where I would have ended up had I not serendipitously found that slim, dusty volume. It opened the door into a world that has forever transformed my life. These quotes are more than just quotes. They represent the very best of the best quotes and ideas from these great leaders that I've read and accumulated over the past three decades. Their voices speak to you from the past, and the present day.

This book is my way of paying it forward if you will. It's a gift to others also hungry for guidance, wisdom, and answers on what it takes to be a great leader. Why just quotes on leadership? It's quite simple really: in the 21st century there is a desperate need for great leadership. Sadly, our society as a whole lacks great leaders. So then, let us become this generation's great leaders.

I hope you find this book helpful on your path. I sincerely would enjoy hearing from you. Feel free to write me at Derek@ TheWisdomOfLeaders.com

Warmly,

Derek Wellington Johnson

# Are you a Great Leader?

Are you a great leader? Do you want to become a great leader? Every one of history's greatest leaders was at one time a neophyte. This book was written to help you become a great leader.

This book is meant to serve as your daily leadership guide. You're welcome to read it straight through, however it was written to be used as a guide for whenever you need advice on a particular aspect of leadership. Imagine being able to ask Alexander The Great a question about strategy, or General Patton about how to inspire loyalty amongst your team, or perhaps having Machiavelli whisper in your ear some sagely advice on how to navigate office politics. Well, now you can.

In his brilliant book "On Leadership" John W. Gardner noted that, "At the time this nation was formed, our population stood at 3 million. And we produced out of that 3 million perhaps six leaders of world class- Washington, Adams, Jefferson, Franklin, Madison and Hamilton. Today our population stands at 322 million, so we might expect at least 106 times as many world class leaders – 638 Jeffersons, Madisons, Adamses, Washingtons, Hamiltons, and Franklins. Where are the Jeffersons and Lincolns of today? The answer, I am convinced, is that they are among us. Out there in settings with which we all familiar are the unawakened leaders, feeling no overpowering call to lead and hardly aware of the potential within."

And to that I would add, let's extrapolate those numbers to a global population of over 7 billion people. Surely there must be thousands of visionary leaders amongst them?

I challenge you to step forward and become one of this century's great leaders. And remember, great leaders aren't born, they're forged.

# PART ONE
# LEADERSHIP AND WINNING

*Caesar Marcus Aurelius Antoninus Augustus*

# CHAPTER ONE

## What makes a Great Leader?

"A great nation is like a great man: When he makes a mistake, he realizes it. Having realized it, he admits it. Having admitted it, he corrects it. He considers those who point out his faults as his most benevolent teachers."

– Lao Tzu

## Aristotle

"He who has never learned to obey cannot be a good commander."

## Mary Kay Ash

"Do not desire to fit in. Desire to lead."

## Marcus Aurelius

"Waste no more time arguing about what a good man should be. Be one."

## Warren G. Bennis

"Managers do things right. Leaders do the right thing."

## Sun Bin

"There is no command without leadership."

## Bill Bradley

"Leadership is unlocking people's potential to become better."

## John Buchan

"The task of leadership is not to put greatness into humanity, but to elicit it, for the greatness is already there."

## Arleigh A. Burke

"Leadership is understanding people and involving them to help you do a job. That takes all of the good characteristics, like integrity, dedication of purpose, selflessness, knowledge, skill, implacability, as well as determination not to accept failure."

## Andrew Carnegie

"No man will make a great leader who wants to do it all himself, or to get all the credit for doing it."

## Chanakya, The Indian Machiavelli

"That ruler stays long in power who acts like a skilled gardener: rehabilitating uprooted ones, watching the blooming ones, strengthening the weak, bending down to the tall ones, weakening the excessively strong ones, separating the clustered ones, trimming the thorny ones, and protecting the ones that have come up by themselves."

## Carl Von Clausewitz

"There has never been a great and distinguished commander of mean intelligence."

## Peter Drucker

"Effective leadership is not about making speeches or being liked; leadership is defined by results not attributes."

"Management is doing things right; leadership is doing the right thing."

"Leadership is not magnetic personality, that can just as well be a glib tongue. It is not "making friends and influencing people," that is flattery. Leadership is lifting a person's vision to higher sights, the raising of a person's performance to a higher standard, the building of a personality beyond its normal limitations."

## Dwight D. Eisenhower

"Leadership consists of nothing but taking responsibility for everything that goes wrong and giving your subordinates credit for everything that goes well."

"I'll tell you what leadership is: It's persuasion ... and conciliation ... and education ... and patience."

"The supreme quality of leadership is integrity."

"Leadership is the art of getting someone else to do something you want done because he wants to do it."

"The supreme quality for leadership is unquestionably integrity. Without it, no real success is possible, no matter whether it is on a section gang, a football field, in an army, or in an office."

> "The first and last task of a leader is to keep hope alive."
>
> – John W. Gardner

## Harold S. Geneen

''I don't believe in just ordering people to do things. You have to sort of grab an oar and row with them. My philosophy is to stay as close as possible to what's happening. If I can't solve something, how the hell can I expect my managers to?"

## Arnold Glasow

"A good leader takes a little more than his share of the blame, a little less than his share of the credit."

## Johann Wolfgang Von Goethe

"A great person attracts great people and knows how to hold them together."

## B. H. Liddell Hart

"A commander should have a profound understanding of human nature, the knack of smoothing out troubles, the power of winning affection while communicating energy, and the capacity for ruthless determination where required by circumstances. He needs to generate an electrifying current, and to keep a cool head in applying it."

## Dee Hock

"If you don't understand that you work for your mislabeled 'subordinates', then you know nothing of leadership. You know only tyranny."

*Johann Wolfgang Von Goethe*

## Tokugawa Ieyasu

"The strong manly ones in life are those who understand the meaning of the word patience. Patience means restraining one's inclinations. There are seven emotions: joy, anger, anxiety, adoration, grief, fear, and hate, and if a man does not give way to these he can be called patient. I am not as strong as I might be, but I have long known and practiced patience. And if my descendants wish to be as I am, they must study patience."

## Steve Jobs

"Innovation distinguishes between a leader and a follower."

## John F. Kennedy

"Leadership and learning are indispensable to each other."

[Undelivered remarks for Dallas Trade Mart, November 22 1963]

## Martin Luther King Jr.

"A genuine leader is not a searcher for consensus but a molder of consensus."

**Ray Kroc**

"I guess to be an entrepreneur you have to have a large ego, enormous pride and an ability to inspire others to follow your lead."

**Tom Landry**

"Leadership is getting someone to do what they don't want to do, to achieve what they want to achieve."

"Nearly all men can stand adversity, but if you want to test a man's character, give him power."

– Abraham Lincoln

## Titus Livy

"What was needed was not merely a resolute man, but a man who was also free from the net of legal controls. Such being the circumstances, Quinctius declared that he would nominate Lucius Quinctius Cincinnatus as Dictator, convinced that in him were courage and resolution equal to the majestic authority of that office. The proposal was unanimously approved, but Cincinnatus, hesitating to accept the burden of responsibility, asked what the Senate was thinking of to wish to expose an old man like him to what must prove the sternest of struggles; but hesitation was in vain, for when from every corner of the House came the cry that in that aged heart lay more wisdom – yes, and courage too – than in all the rest put together, and when praises, well deserved, were heaped upon him and the consul refused to budge an inch from his purpose, Cincinnatus gave way and, with a prayer to God to save his old age from bringing loss or dishonor upon his country in her trouble, was named Dictator by the consul."

– Titus Livy, The Early History of Rome.

## Vince Lombardi Jr.

"Leaders aren't born, they are made. They are made by hard effort, which is the price which all of us must pay to achieve any goal which is worthwhile."

## Niccolò Machiavelli

"He who wishes to be obeyed must know how to command."

"A prudent man should always follow in the path trodden by great men and imitate those who are most excellent, so that if he does not attain to their greatness, at any rate he will get some tinge of it."

*Niccolò Machiavelli*

## Nelson Mandela

"A leader ... is like a shepherd. He stays behind the flock, letting the most nimble go out ahead, whereupon the others follow, not realizing that all along they are being directed from behind."

## Donald H. McGannon

"Leadership is an action, not a position."

## George J. Mecherle

"A man has to live and sleep with his business if he wants to make a go of it. You have to take it home with you at night, so you can lie there in the darkness and figure out what you can do to improve it. In fact, you have to become sort of a "nut" about it, so that you become so enthused that you will bore your friends talking about it. You have to be a one-man crusade."

## Bernard Montgomery

"My own definition of leadership is this: The capacity and the will to rally men and women to a common purpose and the character which inspires confidence."

**Larry Page**

"My job as a leader is to make sure everybody in the company has great opportunities, and that they feel they're having a meaningful impact and are contributing to the good of society. As a world, we're doing a better job of that. My goal is for Google to lead, not follow that."

**Theodore Roosevelt**

"People ask the difference between a leader and a boss... The leader works in the open, and the boss in covert. The leader leads, and the boss drives."

"The three essential qualities of leadership are integrity, the ability to inspire, and above all, insight."

– Sadhguru

## Charles M. Schwab

"I consider my ability to arouse enthusiasm among men the greatest asset I possess."

## James Stockdale

"Leadership must be based on goodwill. Goodwill does not mean posturing and, least of all, pandering to the mob. It means obvious and wholehearted commitment to helping followers."

## Jiang Taigong

"If the general is not benevolent, then the army will not be close to or support him. If the general is not courageous, then the army will not be fierce. If the general is not wise, then the army will be in doubts. If the general is not perspicacious, then the army will be confounded. If the general is not quick-witted and acute, then the army will lose the opportunity. If the general is not constantly alert, the army will be weak in defense. If the general is not strong and forceful, then the army will fail in their duty. Thus the general is the Master of Fate. The army is ordered because of him, and they are disordered because of him as well. If one obtains someone who is worthy to serve as general, the army will be strong and the state will prosper. If one does not obtain a worthy as general, the army will be weak and state will perish."

## Robert Townsend

"A leader is not an administrator who loves to run others, but someone who carries water for his people so that they can get on with their jobs."

## Wu Qi

"Courage is but one of the many required characteristics of a general. Being only courageous, one would rashly rush into battle without any consideration for the gains and loss. Such action is not acceptable."

## Fred Smith

"A manager is not a person who can do the work better than his men; he is a person who can get his men to do the work better than he can."

"Leadership is simply the ability of an individual to coalesce the efforts of other individuals toward achieving common goals. It boils down to looking after your people and ensuring that, from top to bottom, everyone feels part of the team."

## Harry S. Truman

"Men make history and not the other way around. In periods where there is no leadership, society stands still. Progress occurs when courageous, skillful leaders seize the opportunity to change things for the better."

## William Wallace

"He was a tall man with the body of a giant, cheerful in appearance with agreeable features ... but with a wild look ... a most spirited fighting man, with all his limbs very strong and firm. He was most liberal in all his gifts, very fair in his judgments, most compassionate in comforting the sad, a most skillful counselor, very patient when suffering, a distinguished speaker, who above all hunted down falsehood and deceit and treachery."

– Description of Sir William Wallace.

## Jeff Weiner

"Inspire, empower, listen and appreciate. Practicing any one of these can improve employee engagement; mastering all four can change the game."

## Jack Welch

"When you become a leader success is all about growing others."

## Arthur Wellesley – The Duke of Wellington

"...the quality I wish to see the officers possess who are at the head of the troops is a cool discriminating judgment in action, which will enable them to decide with promptitude how far they can go, and ought to go with propriety; and to act with such vigor and decision, that the soldiers will look up to them with confidence in the moment of action, and obey them with alacrity."

## John "Jocko" Willink

"Extreme Ownership. Leaders must own everything in their world. There is no one else to blame."

*Aristotle*

# CHAPTER TWO

## On Making Fast, Powerful and Effective Decisions

"Making good decisions is a crucial skill at every level."

– Peter Drucker

## Aristotle

"For when a thing is known and judged, there is no longer any need of argument."

"It is the mark of an educated mind to be able to entertain a thought without accepting it."

## Marcus Aurelius

"If any man is able to convince me and show me that I do not think or act rightly, I will gladly change; for I seek the truth, by which no man was ever injured. But he is injured who abides in his error and ignorance."

## Bernard M. Baruch

"Whatever failures I have known, whatever errors I have committed, whatever follies I have witnessed in public and private life, have been the consequences of action without thought."

## Jeff Bezos

"Most decisions should probably be made with somewhere around 70% of the information you wish you had. If you wait for 90%, in most cases, you're probably being slow. Plus, either way, you need to be good at quickly recognizing and correcting bad decisions. If you're good at course correcting, being wrong may be less costly than you think, whereas being slow is going to be expensive for sure."

## John Boyd

Air Force Colonel John Boyd is considered one of the 20th Century's greatest military geniuses. His nickname was "40 Second Boyd," because he could defeat any fighter pilot from a disadvantaged position in less than 40 seconds. The legend is that he never lost a dog fight. Ever. Thankfully, Boyd was able to break down exactly what he did and train others on what he called the OODA Loop. OODA stands for Observe, Orient, Decide, and Act.

"In combat the process looked like this:
Observe the enemy and notice their actions
Orient yourself to the situation and move to a better position
Decide on best course of action
Act with speed and intensity."

"The key is to obscure your intentions and make them unpredictable to your opponent while you simultaneously clarify his intentions. That is, operate at a faster tempo to generate rapidly changing conditions that inhibit your opponent from adapting or reacting to those changes and that suppress or destroy his awareness.

Thus, a hodgepodge of confusion and disorder occur to cause him to over- or under-react to conditions or activities that appear to be uncertain, ambiguous, or incomprehensible." – Harry Hillaker, one of Boyd's colleagues, July 1997 issue of Code One magazine, published by Lockheed Martin Tactical Aircraft System.

"He who can handle the quickest rate of change survives."

> "We know what happens to people who stay in the middle of the road. They get run down."
>
> – Aneurin Bevan

**Richard Branson**

"Only a fool never changes his mind."

## Carl von Clausewitz

"In tactics every engagement, great or small, is a defensive one if we leave the initiative to the enemy."

"Pursue one great decisive aim with force and determination."

"Never forget that no military leader has ever become great without audacity. If the leader is filled with high ambition and if he pursues his aims with audacity and strength of will, he will reach them in spite of all obstacles."

## Cicero

"Men decide far more problems by hate, love, lust, rage, sorrow, joy, hope, fear, illusion or some other inward emotion, than by reality, authority, any legal standard, judicial precedent, or statute."

## Michael Dell

"One of the things I benefited from when I started this business was that I didn't know anything. I was just instinct with no preconceived notions. This enabled me to learn and change quickly without having to worry about maintaining any kind of status quo, like some of my bigger competitors."

## Dwight D. Eisenhower

"No man can always be right. So the struggle is to do one's best; to keep the brain and conscience clear; never to be swayed by unworthy motives or inconsequential reasons, but to strive to unearth the basic factors involved, then do one's duty."

"I know of only one way in which you can be sure you have done your best to make a wise decision. That is to get all of the [responsible policymakers] with their different viewpoints in front of you, and listen to them debate. I do not believe in bringing them in one at a time, and therefore being more impressed by the most recent one you hear than the earliest ones. You must get courageous men of strong views, and let them debate with each other."

"It is far more important to be able to hit the target than it is to haggle over who makes a weapon or who pulls a trigger."

## Epictetus

"It is impossible for a man to learn what he thinks he already knows."

**Carlos Ghosn**

"The role of leadership is to transform the complex situation into small pieces and prioritize them."

**Ulysses S. Grant**

"Everyone has his superstitions. One of mine has always been when I started to go anywhere, or to do anything, never to turn back or to stop until the thing intended was accomplished."

"I will either find a way, or make one."

– Hannibal

## Dag Hammarskjold

"Never for the sake of peace and quiet deny your own experience and convictions."

## Patrick Henry

"I have but one lamp by which my feet are guided, and that is the lamp of experience. I know of no way of judging the future but by the past."

## Lee Iacocca

"If I had to sum up in one word what makes a good manager I'd say decisiveness. You can use the fanciest computers to gather the numbers, but in the end you have to set the timetable and act."

"So what do we do? Anything. Something. So long as we don't just sit there. If we screw it up, start over. Try something else. If we wait until we've satisfied all the uncertainties, it may be too late."

## William James

"The art of being wise is the art of knowing what to overlook."

## Herb Kelleher

"It is my practice to try to understand how valuable something is by trying to imagine myself without it."

## Douglas MacArthur

"Once war is forced upon us, there is no alternative than to apply every available means to bring it to a swift end. War's very object is victory – not prolonged indecision."

"It is fatal to enter any war without the will to win it."

## Niccolò Machiavelli

"You must never believe that the enemy does not know how to conduct his own affairs. Indeed, if you want to be deceived less and want to bear less danger, the more the enemy is weak or the less the enemy is cautious, so much more must you esteem him."

## George Catlett Marshall, Jr

"When a thing is done, it's done. Don't look back. Look forward to your next objective."

## Miyamoto Musashi

"Everything can collapse. Houses, bodies, and enemies collapse when their rhythm becomes deranged. In large-scale strategy, when the enemy starts to collapse you must pursue him without letting the chance go. If you fail to take advantage of your enemies' collapse, they may recover."

"If you do not look at things on a large scale it will be difficult for you to master strategy."

"In large-scale strategy, it is beneficial to strike at the corners of the enemy's force, If the corners are overthrown, the spirit of the whole body will be overthrown."

## Elon Musk

"Don't delude yourself into thinking something's working when it's not, or you're gonna get fixated on a bad solution."

## Golda Meir

"A leader who does not hesitate before he sends a nation into battle is not fit to be a leader."

## Napoleon I

"War is essentially a calculation of probabilities."

"Take time to deliberate, but when the time for action comes, stop thinking and go in."

"The art of war does not require complicated maneuvers; the simplest are the best, and common sense is fundamental. From which one might wonder how it is generals make blunders; it is because they try to be clever. The most difficult thing is to guess the enemy's plan, to sift the truth from all the reports that come in. The rest merely requires common sense; it is like a boxing match, the more you punch the better it is. It is also necessary to read the map well."

"Nothing is more difficult, and therefore more precious, than to be able to decide."

"In war, there is but one favorable moment; the great art is to seize it!"

## George S. Patton

"A good plan executed today is better than a perfect plan executed at some indefinite point in the future."

## T. Boone Pickens

"Be willing to make decisions. That's the most important quality in a good leader. Don't fall victim to what I call the "ready-aim-aim-aim-aim" syndrome. You must be willing to fire."

"To make no mistakes is not in the power of man; but from their errors and mistakes the wise and good learn wisdom for the future."

– Plutarch

## Eddie Rickenbacker

I can give you a six-word formula for success: Think things through, then follow through."

## Erwin Rommel

"Don't fight a battle if you don't gain anything by winning."

## Herbert Louis Samuel

"Do not choose to be wrong for the sake of being different."

## H. Norman Schwarzkopf, Jr.

"Do what is right, not what you think the high headquarters wants or what you think will make you look good."

"Every great action is extreme when it is undertaken. Only after it has been accomplished does it seem possible to those creatures of more common stuff."

– Stendhal

## Sun Tzu

"Thus we may know that there are five essentials for victory: (1) He will win who knows when to fight and when not to fight. (2) He will win who knows how to handle both superior and inferior forces. (3) He will win whose army is animated by the same spirit throughout all its ranks. (4) He will win who, prepared himself, waits to take the enemy unprepared. (5) He will win who has military capacity and is not interfered with by the sovereign."

## Jiang Taigong

"Thus it is said that if one fights before understanding the situation, even if he is more numerous, he will certainly be defeated."

## Vegetius

"A battle is commonly decided in two or three hours, after which no further hopes are left for the worsted army. Every plan, therefore, is to be considered, every expedient tried and every method taken before matters are brought to this last extremity. Good officers decline general engagements where the danger is common, and prefer the employment of stratagem and finesse to destroy the enemy as much as possible in detail and intimidate them without exposing our own forces."

## Jack Welch

"Effective people know when to stop assessing and make a tough call, even without total information. Little is worse than a manager who can't cut bait."

"Face reality as it is, not as it was or as you wish it to be."

## John Wooden

"It's what you learn after you know it all that counts."

## Wu Qi

"See the possibilities and advance, know the difficulties and withdraw."

## Xenophon

"A cavalry commander should also devise tricks of his own, suitable for his situation. The basic point is that deceit is your most valuable asset in war... If you think about it, you will find that the majority of important military successes have come about as a result of trickery. It follows, then, that if you are to take on the office of commander, you should ask the gods to allow you to count the ability to deceive among your qualifications, and should also work on it yourself."

*General Charles De Gaulle*

# CHAPTER THREE

## On Planning

"Dig a well before you are thirsty."

– Chinese Proverb

## Russell L. Ackoff

"The righter we do the wrong thing, the wronger we become. When we make a mistake doing the wrong thing and correct it, we become wronger. When we make a mistake doing the right thing and correct it, we become righter. Therefore, it is better to do the right thing wrong than the wrong thing right. This is very significant because almost every problem confronting our society is a result of the fact that our public policy makers are doing the wrong things and are trying to do them righter."

## Marcus Aurelius

"Because a thing seems difficult for you, do not think it impossible for anyone to accomplish."

"However beautiful the strategy, you should occasionally look at the results."

– Winston S. Churchill

## Cicero

"Nescire autem quid antequam natus sis acciderit, id est semper esse puerum. (To be ignorant of what occurred before you were born is to remain always a child.)"

"A mind without instruction can no more bear fruit than can a field, however fertile, without cultivation."

## Charles De Gaulle

"The Army became stuck in a set of ideas which had had their heyday before the end of the First World War. It was all the more inclined that way because its leaders were growing old at their posts, wedded to errors that once constituted their glory."

– Charles De Gaulle speaking on France's staggering lack of preparedness for World War II.

## W. Edwards Deming

"Eighty percent of American managers cannot answer with any measure of confidence these seemingly simple questions: What is my job? What in it really counts? How well am I doing?"

"In God we trust; all others bring data."

"A goal without a method is cruel."

"Failure of management to plan for the future and to foresee problems has brought about waste of manpower, of materials, and of machine-time, all of which raise the manufacturer's cost and price that the purchaser must pay. The consumer is not always willing to subsidize this waste. The inevitable result is loss of market. Loss of market begets unemployment."

## Peter Drucker

"There is nothing so useless as doing efficiently that which should not be done at all."

"I will never forget when [Franklin D.] Roosevelt announced that we would build thirty thousand fighter planes. I was on the task force that worked on our economic strength, and we had just reached the conclusion that we could build, at most, four thousand. We thought, "For goodness sake – he's senile!" Two years later we built fifty thousand. I don't know whether he knew, or if he just realized that unless you set objectives very high, you don't achieve anything at all."

– Peter Drucker, in interview with Bill Moyers, 1988.

## Dwight D. Eisenhower

"Neither a wise nor a brave man lies down on the tracks of history to wait for the train of the future to run over him."

"In preparing for battle I have always found that plans are useless, but planning is indispensable."

## Queen Elizabeth I

"If we still advise we shall never do."

## Epictetus

"A ship should not ride on a single anchor, nor life on a single hope"

"First say to yourself what you would be; and then do what you have to do."

"No great thing is created suddenly."

## Benjamin Franklin

"Never confuse motion with action."

"An ounce of prevention is worth a pound of cure."

"Chess teaches foresight, by having to plan ahead; vigilance, by having to keep watch over the whole chess board; caution, by having to restrain ourselves from making hasty moves; and finally, we learn from chess the greatest maxim in life – that even when everything seems to be going badly for us we should not lose heart, but always hoping for a change for the better, steadfastly continue searching for the solutions to our problems."

### Frederick the Great

"Without supplies no army is brave."

### Genghis Khan

"An action committed in anger is an action doomed to failure."

### Johann Wolfgang von Goethe

"He who moves not forward , goes backward."

### Baltasar Gracián

"Readiness is the mother of luck."

**David Hackworth**

"If you find yourself in a fair fight, you didn't plan your mission properly."

**John F. Kennedy**

"There are risks and costs to a program of action, but they are far less than the long range risks and costs of comfortable inaction."

"The map is not the territory."

– Alfred Korzybski

**Abraham Lincoln**

"Give me six hours to chop down a tree and I will spend the first four sharpening the axe."

## Titus Livy

"There is this exceptionally beneficial and fruitful advantage to be derived from the study of the past, that you see, set in the clear light of historical truth, examples of every possible type. From these you may select for yourself and your country what to imitate, and also what, as being mischievous in its inception and disastrous in its issues, you are to avoid."

– Titus Livius, History of Rome.

## Douglas MacArthur

"A good soldier, whether he leads a platoon or an army, is expected to look backward as well as forward, but he must think only forward."

## Modern Military saying

"Amateurs talk tactics, professionals talk logistics."

## Helmuth Karl Bernhard Graf von Moltke

"The tactical result of an engagement forms the base for new strategic decisions because victory or defeat in a battle changes the situation to such a degree that no human acumen is able to see beyond the first battle."

This quote has been paraphrased into, "No plan survives contact with the enemy."

## Miyamoto Musashi

"Do nothing that is of no use"

"It is difficult to understand the universe if you only study one planet"- Miyamoto Musashi, A Book of Five Rings: The Classic Guide to Strategy.

## George S. Patton

"Prepare for the unknown by studying how others in the past have coped with the unforeseeable and the unpredictable."- General George S. Patton.

> "I am more afraid of our own mistakes than of our enemies' designs."
>
> – Pericles

**Military Axiom**

"Two is one, and one is none."
– Military axiom on being adequately prepared for whatever may come your way.

**Erwin Rommel**

"Don't fight a battle if you don't gain anything by winning."

**Franklin D. Roosevelt**

"There are many ways of going forward, but only one way of standing still."

**Sun Tzu**

"Now the general who wins a battle makes many calculations in his temple before the battle is fought. The general who loses a battle makes but few calculations beforehand. Thus do many calculations lead to victory, and few calculations to defeat: How much more no calculation at all! It is by attention to this point that I can see who is likely to win."

"If ignorant both of your enemy and yourself, you are certain to be in peril."

"What is of the greatest importance in war is extraordinary speed: One cannot afford to neglect opportunity."

## Jack Welch

"When you are a leader, your job is to have all the questions. You have to be incredibly comfortable looking like the dumbest person in the room. Every conversation you have about a decision, a proposal, or a piece of market information has to be filled with you saying, "What if?" and "Why not?" and "How come?"

## John Wooden

"When opportunity comes, it's too late to prepare."

## Xenophon

"If we have to fight a battle, what we must see to is how we may fight with the greatest efficiency."

*Benjamin Franklin*

# CHAPTER FOUR

## On Taking Risks

"Pearls don't lie on the seashore. If you want one, you must dive for it."

– Chinese Proverb

## Herbert Casson

"For many years, 'safety first' has been the saying of the human race ... but it has never been the motto of leaders. A leader must face danger, he must take the risk, the blame and face the brunt of the storm."

## Peter Drucker

"The better a man is the more mistakes he will make, for the more new things he will try. I would never promote to a top-level a man who was not making mistakes otherwise I am sure he is a mediocre."

"Whenever you see a successful business, someone once made a courageous decision."

## Benjamin Franklin

"When you're testing to see how deep water is, never use two feet."

## Baltasar Gracian

"Knowledge without courage is sterile."

"Say farewell to luck when winning. It is the way of the gamblers of reputation. Quite as important as a gallant advance is a well-planned retreat. Lock up your winnings when they are enough, or when great. Continuous luck is always suspect; more secure is that which changes. Though half bitter and half sweet, it is more satisfying to the taste. The more luck pyramids, the greater the danger of slip and collapse. For luck always compensates her intensity by her brevity. Fortune wearies of carrying anyone long upon her shoulders."

## Roberto Goizueta

"We become uncompetitive by not being tolerant of mistakes. The moment you let avoiding failure becomes your motivator, you are down the path of inactivity. You can step on your toe if you are moving."
– Former CEO of The Coca-Cola Company, Roberto Goizueta when asked why he rehired the Chief Marketing Officer, Sergio Zyman, who had resigned in disgrace over the failure of the New Coke campaign.

"If you take risks, you may fail. But if you do not take risks, you will surely fail. The greatest risk of all is to do nothing."

## David Loyd George

"Don't be afraid to take a big step when one is indicated. You can't cross a chasm in two small steps."

## Grace Hopper

"If it's a good idea, go ahead and do it. It's much easier to apologize than it is to get permission."

## Admiral John Paul Jones

"It seems to be a law of nature, inflexible and inexorable, that those who will not risk cannot win."

## Douglas MacArthur

"There is no security on this earth; there is only opportunity."

## David Mahoney

"Refuse to join the cautious crowd that plays not to lose. Play to win."

## George S. Patton

"Take calculated risks. This is quite different from being rash."

## Eddie Rickenbacker

"The experienced fighting pilot does not take unnecessary risks. His business is to shoot down enemy planes, not to get shot down."

## Eleanor Roosevelt

"Do one thing every day that scares you."

## Sam Walton

"Many of our best opportunities were created out of necessity."

*Sir Winston Churchill*

# CHAPTER FIVE

## On Handling Crises

> "The Chinese use two brush strokes to write the word 'crisis.' One brush stroke stands for danger; the other for opportunity. In a crisis, be aware of the danger – but recognize the opportunity."
>
> – John F. Kennedy

## Marcus Aurelius

"We shrink from change; yet is there anything that can come into being without it? What does Nature hold dearer, or more proper to herself? Could you have a hot bath unless the firewood underwent some change? ... Is it possible for any useful thing to be achieved without change? Do you not see, then, that change in yourself is of the same order and no less necessary to Nature?"

## David Ben-Gurion

"Courage is a special kind of knowledge: the knowledge of how to fear what ought to be feared and how not to fear what ought not to be feared."

## Warren G. Bennis

"In a time of drastic change, it is the learners who inherit the future. The learned find themselves equipped to live in a world that no longer exists."

## Omar Bradley

"Bravery is the capacity to perform properly even when scared half to death."

## Richard Branson

"I have always believed that the only way to cope with a cash crisis is not to contract but to try to expand out of it."

## Brasidas of Sparta

"Fear makes men forget, and skill which cannot fight is useless."

## Julius Caesar

"When the swords flash, let no idea of love, piety, or even the face of your fathers move you."

## Chanakya, The Indian Machiavelli

"As the tortoise withdraws its limbs, the ruler should try to hide any part of his which might have been exposed."

"Even after winning (a battle) a ruler with a weak army and treasury is a loser."

"A fight between equals, like the collision of one unbaked pot with another, destroys both."

"The people help the ruler who is just in his actions, when attacked while in a serious calamity."

"The one who is facing defeat should make peace."

"Even a small weakness creates trouble."

"The one for whom destruction is imminent does not listen to wholesome advice."

"There is no enemy equal to hunger."

"He whose destruction is imminent plans evil action."

## Winston S. Churchill

"Danger: if you meet it promptly and without flinching, you will reduce the danger by half. Never run away from anything. Never!"

"Success is not final, failure is not fatal: it is the courage to continue that counts."

"As the severity of military operations increases, so also must the sternness of the discipline. The zeal of the soldiers, their warlike instincts, and the interests and excitements of war may ensure obedience of orders and the cheerful endurance of perils and hardships during a short and prosperous campaign. But when fortune is dubious or adverse; when retreats as well as advances are necessary; when supplies fail, arrangements miscarry, and disasters impend, and when the struggle is protracted, men can only be persuaded to accept evil things by the lively realization of the fact that greater terrors await their refusal."

"True genius resides in the capacity for evaluation of uncertain, hazardous and conflicting information."

"Kites rise highest against the wind, not with it."

"The maxim 'Nothing prevails but perfection' may be spelled PARALYSIS."

"Courage is rightly esteemed the first of human qualities, because... it is the quality that guarantees all others."

"Any man can make mistakes, but only an idiot persists in his error."

– Cicero

## Dwight D. Eisenhower

"What counts is not necessarily the size of the dog in the fight – it's the size of the fight in the dog."

## Larry Ellison

"All you can do is every day, try to solve a problem and make your company better. You can't worry about it, you can't panic when you look at the stock market's decline. You get frozen like a deer in the headlights. All you can do is all you can do."

## Epictetus

"On the occasion of every accident that befalls you, remember to turn to yourself and inquire what power you have for turning it to use."

"It's not what happens to you, but how you react to it that matters."

"Man is not worried by real problems so much as by his imagined anxieties about real problems"

"There is only one way to happiness and that is to cease worrying about things which are beyond the power or our will. "

"Difficulty shows what men are."

"...when things seem to have reached that stage, merely say "I won't play any longer", and take your departure; but if you stay, stop lamenting."

"The greater the difficulty, the more glory in surmounting it. Skillful pilots gain their reputation from storms and tempests. "

"Do not anticipate trouble, or worry about what may never happen. Keep in the sunlight."

– Benjamin Franklin

**Viktor E. Frankl**

"Those who have a 'why' to live, can bear with almost any 'how'."

"Life is never made unbearable by circumstances, but only by lack of meaning and purpose."

"Everything can be taken from a man but one thing: the last of the human freedoms – to choose one's attitude in any given set of circumstances, to choose one's own way."

## Arnold Glasow

"One of the tests of leadership is the ability to recognize a problem before it becomes an emergency."

## Baltasar Gracián

"Never do anything when you are in a temper, for you will do everything wrong."

"Two kinds of people are good at foreseeing danger: those who have learned at their own expense, and the clever people who learn a great deal at the expense of others."

## Ulysses S. Grant

"In every battle there comes a time when both sides consider themselves beaten, then he who continues the attack wins."

## Heinz Wilhem Guderian

"There are no desperate situations, there are only desperate people."

## William F. Halsey

"Hit hard, hit fast, hit often."

"Problems, personal, national, or combat, become smaller if you don't dodge them but confront them. Touch a thistle timidly and it pricks you; grasp it boldly, and its spines crumble. Carry the battle to the enemy! Lay your ship alongside his!"

## Patrick Henry

"The battle, sir, is not to the strong alone; it is to the vigilant, the active, the brave."

## Eric Hoffer

"You can discover what your enemy fears most by observing the means he uses to frighten you."

## Special Forces/Delta Operator MSG Paul R. Howe

"If your tactics are sound and you believe that they will keep you relatively safe while delivering devastating fire to your opponent, you will have less fear and apprehension going into harm's way."

## Thomas Jefferson

"The most fortunate of us all in our journey through life frequently meet with calamities and misfortunes which greatly afflict us. To fortify our minds against the attacks of these calamities and misfortunes should be one of the principal studies and endeavors of our lives."

## Steve Jobs

"Sometimes life's going to hit you in the head with a brick. Don't lose faith. I'm convinced that the only thing that kept me going was that I loved what I did."

"You have to be burning with an idea, or a problem, or a wrong that you want to right. If you're not passionate enough from the start, you'll never stick it out."

*Thomas Jefferson*

## John Paul Jones

"I have not yet begun to fight!"
– John Paul Jones's response after the enemy suggested he surrender during the early stages of a ferocious 3.5 hour gun battle. He ended up winning this brutal sea battle.

## Robert F. Kennedy

"Few men are willing to brave the disapproval of their fellows, the censure of their colleagues, the wrath of their society. Moral courage is a rarer commodity than bravery in battle or great intelligence. Yet it is the one essential, vital quality for those who seek to change a world which yields most painfully to change."

"When your hopes and dreams and goals are dashed, search among the wreckage, you may find a golden opportunity hidden in the ruins."

– A. P. J. Abdul Kalam

## Titus Livy

"In difficult and desperate situations, the boldest plans are the safest."

## Abraham Lincoln

"You cannot escape the responsibility of tomorrow by evading it today."

"My great concern is not whether you have failed, but whether you are content with your failure."

"If I were to try and read, much less answer, the attacks made on me, this shop might as well be closed for any other business. I do the very best that I know how, the very best way I can, and I mean to keep on doing so until the end. If the end brings me out all right, then what is said against me won't matter. If the end brings me out wrong, then ten angels swearing I was right would make no difference."

## Vince Lombardi Jr.

"The real glory is being knocked to your knees and then coming back. That's real glory. That's the essence of it."

"In great attempts it is glorious even to fail."

## Jim Lovell

"...you have to have a positive attitude, number one. And number two, we were all from test pilot backgrounds, so naturally, this was an adventure. [With Apollo 13] we had to say, "Okay, here's the problem. What do we have to work with? Is it immediate that we have to do something?" We first thought a meteorite had hit the Lunar Module. Had that happened, we'd have been dead in just a few minutes when we lost atmosphere. But that wasn't the case. It turned out that the explosion had crippled the Command Module. So we still had the Lunar Module, which we used as a lifeboat to get home."

"I don't worry about crises anymore. I realize that I'm living on borrowed time. Take things in single steps, work toward solutions."

## Clare Boothe Luce

"There are no hopeless situations; there are only men who have grown hopeless about them."

## Jack Ma

"The lessons I learned from the dark days at Alibaba are that you've got to make your team have value, innovation, and vision. Also, if you don't give up, you still have a chance. And, when you are small, you have to be very focused and rely on your brain, not your strength."

## Harvey MacKay

"Even when change is elective, it will disorient you. You may go through anxiety. You will miss aspects of your former life. It doesn't matter. The trick is to know in advance of making any big change that you're going to be thrown off your feet by it. So you prepare for this inevitable disorientation and steady yourself to get through it. Then you take the challenge, make the change, and achieve your dream."

## Niccolò Machiavelli

"Everything that occurs in the world, in every epoch, has something that corresponds to it in ancient times."

## Nelson Mandela

"Quitting is leading too."

"Resentment is like drinking poison and then hoping it will kill your enemies."

"I learned that courage was not the absence of fear, but the triumph over it. The brave man is not he who does not feel afraid, but he who conquers that fear."

## George C. Marshall

"Don't fight the problem. Decide it."

## Dr. Charles Mayo

"Worry affects the circulation, the heart, the glands, the whole nervous system, and profoundly affects the health. I have never known a man who died from overwork, but many who died from doubt."

## Audie Murphy

"Seems to me that if you're afraid or living with some big fear, you're not really living. You're only half alive. I don't care if it's the boss you're scared of or a lot of people in a room or diving off of a dinky little board, you gotta get rid of it. You owe it to yourself. Makes sort of a zombie out of you, being afraid. I mean you want to be free, don't you? And how can you if you are scared? That's prison. Fear's a jailer. Mind now, I'm not a professor on the subject. I just found it out for myself. But that's what I think."

## Miyamoto Musashi

"When in a fight to the death, one wants to employ all one's weapons to the utmost. I must say that to die with

one's sword still sheathed is most regrettable."
– Miyamoto Musashi, 'A Book of Five Rings: The Classic Guide to Strategy'.

## Joe Namath

"I think that at some point in your life you realize you don't have to worry if you do everything you're supposed to do right. Or if not right, if you do it the best you can... what can worry do for you? You are already doing the best you can."

## Napoleon I

"The battlefield is a scene of constant chaos. The winner will be the one who controls that chaos, both his own and the enemies."

"Circumstances – what are circumstances? I make circumstances."

"He who fears being conquered is sure of defeat."

"Courage isn't having the strength to go on – it is going on when you don't have strength."

*Thomas Paine*

## Thomas Paine

"I love the man who can smile in trouble, who can gather strength from distress, and grow brave by reaction. 'Tis the business of little minds to shrink, but he whose heart is firm, and whose conscience approves his conduct, will pursue his principles unto death."

## George S. Patton

"Pressure makes diamonds."

"Success is how high you bounce when you hit bottom."

"Battle is an orgy of disorder. No level lawns or marker flags exist to aid us strut ourselves in vain display, but rather groups of weary wandering men seek gropingly for means to kill their foe. The sudden change from accustomed order to utter disorder – to chaos, but emphasize the folly of schooling to precision and obedience where only fierceness and habituated disorder are useful."

"If we take the generally accepted definition of bravery as a quality which knows no fear, I have never seen a brave man. All men are frightened. The more intelligent they are, the more they are frightened."

"Accept the challenges so that you can feel the exhilaration of victory."

"If you are going to win any battle, you have to do one thing. You have to make the mind run the body. Never let the body tell the mind what to do... the body is never tired if the mind is not tired."

**H. Ross Perot**

"Most people give up just when they're about to achieve success. They quit on the one yard line. They give up at the last minute of the game one foot from a winning touchdown."

"In the war between falsehood and truth, falsehood wins the first battle and truth the last."

– Mujibur Rahman

**Jeannette Rankin**

"What one decides to do in crisis depends on one's philosophy of life, and that philosophy cannot be changed by an incident. If one hasn't any philosophy in crises, others make the decision."

## Erwin Rommel

"Mortal danger is an effective antidote for fixed ideas."

"In a man-to-man fight, the winner is he who has one more round in his magazine."

## Eleanor Roosevelt

"You gain strength, courage and confidence by every experience in which you really stop to look fear in the face. You must do the thing you think you cannot do."

## Franklin D. Roosevelt

"When you reach the end of your rope, tie a knot in it and hang on."

## Theodore Roosevelt

"Do what you can, with what you have, where you are."-

"Nothing in the world is worth having or worth doing unless it means effort, pain, difficulty... I have never in my life envied a human being who led an easy life. I have envied a great many people who led difficult lives and led them well."

## Eddie Rickenbacker

"I believe that if you think about disaster, you will get it. Brood about death and you will hasten your demise. Think positively and masterfully with confidence and faith, and life becomes more secure, more fraught with action, richer in achievement and experience. This is the sure way to win victories over inner defeat. It is the way a humble person meets life or death."

"Courage is doing what you're afraid to do. There can be no courage unless you're scared."

"Keep your fears to yourself, but share your courage with others."

– Robert Louis Stevenson

## James Stockdale

"A properly educated leader, especially when harassed and under pressure, will know from his study of history and the classics that circumstances very much like those he is encountering have occurred from time to time on this earth since the beginning of history. He will avoid the self-indulgent error of seeing himself in a predicament so unprecedented, so unique, as to justify his making an exception to law, custom or morality in favor of himself. The making of such exceptions has been the theme of public life throughout much of our lifetimes. For twenty years, we've been surrounded by gamesmen unable to cope with the wisdom of the ages. They make exceptions to law and custom in favor of themselves because they choose to view ordinary dilemmas as unprecedented crises."

When asked about who died during years of captivity as a prisoner of war in Vietnam: "Oh, that's easy, the optimists. Oh, they were the ones who said, 'We're going to be out by Christmas.' And Christmas would come, and Christmas would go. Then they'd say, 'We're going to be out by Easter.' And Easter would come, and Easter would go. And then Thanksgiving, and then it would be Christmas again. And they died of a broken heart."

## Herbert Swope

"I cannot give you the formula for success, but I can

give you the formula for failure, which is: Try to please everybody."

## Publilius Syrus

"Anyone can hold the helm when the sea is calm."

## Tacitus

"The desire for safety stands against every great and noble enterprise."

## George Washington

"Real men despise battle, but will never run from it."

"The turning points of lives are not the great moments. The real crises are often concealed in occurrences so trivial in appearance that they pass unobserved."

## Thomas J. Watson Jr.

"If you stand up and be counted, from time to time you may get yourself knocked down. But remember this: A man flattened by an opponent can get up again. A man flattened by conformity stays down for good."

## Jack Welch

"It sounds awful, but a crisis rarely ends without blood on the floor. That's not easy or pleasant. But sadly, it is often necessary so the company can move forward again."

## John Wooden

"Ninety percent of the time, the game is going to be decided in the final five minutes. When two teams are evenly matched, the better conditioned team will usually execute better when fatigue sets in, and will probably win."

## Xenophon

"You are well aware that it is not numbers or strength that bring the victories in war. No, it is when one side goes against the enemy with the gods' gift of a stronger morale that their adversaries, as a rule, cannot withstand them. I have noticed this point, too, my friends, that in soldiering, the people whose one aim is to keep alive usually find a wretched and dishonorable death, while the people who, realizing that death is the common lot of all men, make it their endeavor to die with honor, somehow seem more often to reach old age and to have a happier life while they are alive."

## Invictus by William Ernest Henley

Out of the night that covers me,
　　Black as the pit from pole to pole,
I thank whatever gods may be
　　For my unconquerable soul.

In the fell clutch of circumstance
　　I have not winced nor cried aloud.
Under the bludgeonings of chance
　　My head is bloody, but unbowed.

Beyond this place of wrath and tears
　　Looms but the horror of the shade,
And yet the menace of the years
　　Finds and shall find me unafraid.

It matters not how strait the gate,
　　How charged with punishments the scroll,
I am the master of my fate,
　　I am the captain of my soul.

# CHAPTER SIX

## On Outmaneuvering
## Your Competition

"Let your plans be dark and impenetrable as night, and when you move, fall like a thunderbolt."

– Sun Tzu, The Art of War

## Robert Baden-Powell

"In war, you must be prepared for what is possible, not only what is probable."

## Tsukahara Bokuden

"My art is different than yours; it consists not in defeating others, but in not being defeated."

## Richard Branson

"I have always found it to be one of the more intriguing idiosyncrasies of the human condition that a problem that is handled quickly and effectively will almost always serve to generate more long-term customer loyalty than when the original service was delivered satisfactorily."

## Nolan Bushnell

"Putting a spoke in the wheels of my competition has always been part of my philosophy."

"[On Atari] This was a company started with $250. We never had any capital. But we learned that stealth and guile can sometimes work instead."

## Catherine the Great

"I have no way to defend my borders but to extend them."

*Catherine the Great*

## Chanakya, The Indian Machiavelli

"Till the enemy's weakness is known, he should be kept on friendly terms."

In daytime, the crow kills the owl. At night, the owl kills the crow. (The time of the fight is important.) The dog on land drags the crocodile. The crocodile in water drags the dog. (The place of the fight is important.)

"Greed clouds the intellect."

"Power is the cause for the forging of treaties. Unheated metal does not join with metal."

"Feeding a snake with milk increases its venom, no nectar is produced."

"Iron should be cut by iron."

"As a bird is captured by a bait in the form of a bird, enemies should be destroyed by creating trust and offering a bait."

"When there are many enemies, treaty should be entered with one."

"Bees do not go to the flowerless mango tree."

"Even the fangless serpent should raise its hood, for with or without poison, a raised hood is frightening."

"The one who knows the cow's nature gets the milk."

"A good quality should be learnt even from an enemy."

## Winston Churchill

"You will never reach your destination if you stop and throw stones at every dog that barks."

"Difficulties mastered are opportunities won."

## Cicero

"It is not by muscle, speed, or physical dexterity that great things are achieved, but by reflection, force of character, and judgment."

## Carl von Clausewitz

"Given the same amount of intelligence, timidity will do a thousand times more damage than audacity."

"The best form of defense is attack."

"No one starts a war-or rather, no one in his senses ought to do so-without first being clear in his mind what he intends to achieve by that war and how he intends to conduct it."

"If the enemy is to be coerced, you must put him in a situation that is even more unpleasant than the sacrifice you call on him to make. The hardships of the situation must not be merely transient – at least not in appearance. Otherwise, the enemy would not give in, but would wait for things to improve."

"The first and most important rule to observe... is to use our entire forces with the utmost energy. The second rule is to concentrate our power as much as possible against that section where the chief blows are to be delivered and to incur disadvantages elsewhere, so that our chances of success may increase at the decisive point. The third rule is never to waste time. Unless important advantages are to be gained from hesitation, it is necessary to set to work at once. By this speed a hundred enemy measures are nipped in the bud, and public opinion is won most rapidly. Finally, the fourth rule is to follow up our successes with the utmost energy. Only pursuit of the beaten enemy gives the fruits of victory."

"In reviewing the whole array of factors a general must weigh before making his decision, we must remember that he can gauge the direction and value of the most important ones only by considering numerous other possibilities – some immediate, some remote. He must guess, so, to speak: guess whether the first shock of battle will steel the enemy's resolve and stiffen his resistance, or whether, like a Bologna flask, it will shatter as soon as its surface is scratched; guess the extent of debilitation and paralysis that the drying up of particular sources of supply and the severing of certain lines of communication will cause in the enemy; guess whether the burning pain of an injury he has dealt will make the enemy collapse with exhaustion or, like a wounded bull, arouse his rage; guess whether the other powers will be frightened or indignant, and whether and which political alliances will be dissolved or formed. When we realize that he must hit upon all this and much more by means of his discreet judgment, as a marksman hits a target, we must admit that such an accomplishment of the human mind is no small achievement. Thousands of wrong turns running in all directions tempt his perception; and if the range, confusion and complexity of the issues are not enough to overwhelm him, the dangers and responsibilities may."

*Carl Philipp Gottfried von Clausewitz*

## Michael Dell

"I believe that you have to understand the economics of a business before you have a strategy, and you have to understand your strategy before you have a structure. If you get these in the wrong order, you will probably fail."

## W. Edwards Deming

"A dissatisfied customer does not complain: he just switches."

## Larry Ellison

"If you do everything that everyone else does in business, you're going to lose. The only way to really be ahead, is to 'be different'."

## Henry Ford

"The competitor to be feared is one who never bothers about you at all but goes on making his own business better all the time."

## Benjamin Franklin

"An investment in knowledge always pays the best interest."

## Frederick the Great

"Great advantage is drawn from knowledge of your adversary, and when you know the measure of his intelligence and character you can use it to play on his weaknesses."

"War is a science for those who are outstanding; an art for mediocrities; a trade for ignoramuses."

> "Never compete with someone who has nothing to lose."
>
> – Baltasar Gracián

## Roberto Goizueta

"We don't know how to sell products based on performance. Everything we sell, we sell on image."

## Basil Liddell Hart

"Battle should no longer resemble a bludgeon fight, but should be a test of skill, a maneuver combat, in which is fulfilled the great principle of surprise by striking 'from an unexpected direction against an unguarded spot.'"

"Philosophers and scientists have shown that adaptation is the secret of existence. History, however, is a catalogue of failures to change in time with the need. And armies, which because of their role should be the most adaptable of institutions, have been the most rigid – to the cost of the causes they upheld. Almost every great soldier of the past has borne witness to this truth. But it needs no such personal testimony, for the facts of history, unhappily, prove it in overwhelming array. No one can in honesty ignore them if he has once examined them. And to refrain from emphasizing them would be a crime against the country. For it amounts to complicity after the event, which is even more culpable when the life of a people, not merely of one person, is concerned. In the latter case there may be some excuse for discreet silence, as your testimony cannot restore the dead person to life. But in the former case there is no such excuse – because the life of a people will again be at stake in the future."

"But time and surprise are the two most vital elements in war."

"The most consistently successful commanders, when faced by an enemy in a position that was strong naturally or materially, have hardly ever tackled it in a direct way. And when, under pressure of circumstances, they have risked a direct attack, the result has commonly been to blot their record with a failure."

"It is thus more potent, as well as more economical, to disarm the enemy than to attempt his destruction by hard fighting ... A strategist should think in terms of paralyzing, not of killing."

"To ensure attaining an objective, one should have alternate objectives. An attack that converges on one point should threaten, and be able to diverge against another. Only by this flexibility of aim can strategy be attuned to the uncertainty of war. "

"Respecting your opponent is the key to winning any bout. Hold your enemy in contempt and you may miss the strategy behind his moves"

– David Hackworth

## Herodotus

"On the Spartan side, it was a memorable fight; they were men who understood war pitted against an inexperienced enemy, and amongst the feints they employed was to turn their backs in a body and pretend to be retreating in confusion, whereupon the enemy would come on with a great clatter and roar, supposing the battle won; but the Spartans, just as the Persians were on them, would wheel and face them, and inflict in the struggle innumerable casualties."

Greek historian Herodotus, describing the battle of Thermopylae when 300 Spartan warriors valiantly fought thousands of Persians to the last man.

"Carpe diem, quam minimum credula postero."

Translated as, "Seize today, and put as little trust as you can in tomorrow."

– Horace

*The statue of Herodotus at his birthplace Halicarnassus*

## Eric Hoffer

"In times of change, learners inherit the earth, while the learned find themselves beautifully equipped to deal with a world that no longer exists."

## Special Forces/Delta Operator MSG Paul R. Howe

"...defense does not win personal or collective battles."

## Tony Hsieh

"It starts with what customers first see when they visit our website. We offer free shipping both ways to make the transaction as easy as possible and risk-free for our customers. A lot of customers will order five different pairs of shoes, try them on with five different outfits in the comfort of their living rooms, and then send back the ones that don't fit or they simply don't like, free of charge. The additional shipping costs are expensive for us, but we really view those costs as a marketing expense. We offer a 365-day return policy for people who have trouble committing or making up their minds. At most websites, the contact information is usually buried at least five links deep and even when you find it, it's a form or e-mail address that you can only contact once. We take the opposite approach. We put our phone number at the top of every single page, because we actually want to talk to our customers, and we staff our call center 24/7."

## Stonewall Jackson

"Always mystify, mislead, and surprise the enemy, if possible; and when you strike and overcome him, never give up the pursuit as long as your men have strength to follow; for an army routed, if hotly pursued, becomes panic-stricken, and can then be destroyed by half their number."

## Jiang Taigong

"Do not assume that having the numerical advantage, we can treat the enemy lightly."

## John Paul Jones

"Whoever can surprise well must conquer."

## Herb Kelleher

"The core of our success; that's the most difficult thing for a competitor to imitate. They can buy all the physical things. The things you can't buy are dedication, devotion, loyalty, the feeling that you are participating in a crusade."

"When someone comes to me with a cost saving idea, I don't immediately jump up and say yes. I ask: what's the effect on the customer?"

**Ray Kroc**

"You must perfect every fundamental of your business if you expect it to perform well."

> "The printing press is the greatest weapon in the armory of the modern commander."
>
> – T. E. Lawrence

**Jack Ma**

"You should learn from your competitor, but never copy. Copy and you die."

*T. E. Lawrence*

## Niccolò Machiavelli

"The lion cannot protect himself from traps, and the fox cannot defend himself from wolves. One must therefore be a fox to recognize traps, and a lion to frighten wolves."

"No proceeding is better than that which you have concealed from the enemy until the time you have executed it. To know how to recognize an opportunity in war, and take it, benefits you more than anything else. Nature creates few men brave; industry and training makes many. Discipline in war counts more than fury."

"Never attempt to win by force what can be won by deception."

"Nothing is more worthy of the attention of a good general than the endeavor to penetrate the designs of the enemy."

## Harvey MacKay

"One mistake will never kill you. The same mistake over and over again will."

## Nelson Mandela

"When the water starts boiling it is foolish to turn off the heat."

"There are few misfortunes in this world that you cannot turn into a personal triumph if you have the iron will and the necessary skill."

"Know your enemy; and learn about his favorite sport."

## Richard "Dick" Marcinko

"To win, you take the initiative. You instigate the action. You make the opponent react to you."

## The Emperor Maurice

"It is better to avoid a tricky opponent than one who never lets up. The latter makes no secret of what he is doing, whereas it is difficult to find out what the other is up to."

## Miyamoto Musashi

"Immature strategy is the cause of grief."

"You must understand that there is more than one path to the top of the mountain."

"You should not have a favorite weapon. To become over-familiar with one weapon is as much a fault as not knowing it sufficiently well."

"You win battles with the timing in the void born of the timing of cunning by knowing the enemies' timing, and thus using a timing which the enemy does not expect."

"In the strategy of my school, keep your body and mind straight and make your opponent go through contortions and twist about. The essence is to defeat him in the moment when, in his mind, he is pivoting and twisting. You should examine this well."

## Elon Musk

"Sometimes the customer doesn't actually know what they need."

## Napoleon I

"You must not fight too often with one enemy, or you will teach him all your art of war."

"In war one sees his own troubles and not those of the enemy."

"Four hostile newspapers were more to be feared than a thousand bayonets."

"One must change one's tactics every ten years if one wishes to maintain one's superiority."

"Never interrupt your enemy when he is making a mistake."

**Navy SEAL Creed**

"The more you sweat in peace, the less you bleed in war."

"It is often easier to make progress on mega-ambitious dreams. Since no one else is crazy enough to do it, you have little competition."

– Larry Page

**George S. Patton Jr.**

"Battles are won by frightening the enemy. Fear is induced by inflicting death and wounds on him. Death and wounds are produced by fire. Fire from the rear is more deadly and three times more effective than fire from the front, but to get fire behind the enemy, you must hold him by frontal fire and move rapidly around his flank."

"Infantry must move forward to close with the enemy. It must shoot in order to move... To halt under fire is folly. To halt under fire and not fire back is suicide. Officers must set the example."

## H. Ross Perot

"Most people give up just when they're about to achieve success. They quit on the one-yard line. They give up at the last minute of the game, one foot from a winning touchdown."

## Polybius

"A good general not only sees the way to victory; he also knows when victory is impossible."

## Rommel

"It is also greatly in the commander's own interest to have a personal picture of the front and a clear idea of the problems his subordinates are having to face. It is the only way in which he can keep his ideas permanently up to date and adapted to changing conditions. If he fights his battles as a game of chess, he will become rigidly fixed in academic theory and admiration of his own ideas. Success comes most readily to the commander whose ideas have not been canalized into any one fixed channel, but can develop freely from the conditions around him."

## Charles M. Schwab

"Keeping a little ahead of conditions is one of the secrets of business; the trailer seldom goes far."

## Sun Tzu

"Those who are first on the battlefield and await the opponents are at ease; those who are last on the battlefield and head into a fight become exhausted. Therefore, good warriors cause others to go to them and do not go to others."

"In conflict, straightforward actions generally lead to engagement, surprising actions generally lead to victory."

"All warfare is based on deception. Hence, when able to attack, we must seem unable; when using our forces we must seem inactive; when we are near, we must make the enemy believe that we are away; when far away, we must make him believe we are near. Hold out baits to entice the enemy. Feign disorder, and crush him. If he is secure at all points, be prepared for him. If he is in superior strength, evade him. If your opponent is of choleric temper, seek to irritate him. Pretend to be weak, that he may grow arrogant. If he is taking his ease, give him no rest. If his forces are united, separate them. Attack him where he is unprepared, appear where you are not expected."

"He who knows when he can fight and when he cannot, will be victorious."

"Thus, what is of supreme importance in war is to attack the enemy's strategy."

"Strategy without tactics is the slowest route to victory. Tactics without strategy is the noise before defeat."

"All men can see these tactics whereby I conquer, but what none can see is the strategy out of which victory is evolved."

"Military tactics are like unto water; for water in its natural course runs away from high places and hastens downwards. So in war, the way is to avoid what is strong and to strike at what is weak. Water shapes its course according to the nature of the ground over which it flows; the soldier works out his victory in relation to the foe whom he is facing. Therefore, just as water retains no constant shape, so in warfare there are no constant conditions. He who can modify his tactics in relation to his opponent and thereby succeed in winning, may be called a heaven-born captain."

"Let your rapidity be that of the wind, your compactness that of the forest. In raiding and plundering be like fire; in immovability like a mountain. Let your plans be dark and impenetrable as night, and when you move, fall like a thunderbolt."

"Do not interfere with an army that is returning home. When you surround an army, leave an outlet free. Do not press a desperate foe too hard. Such is the art of warfare."

"To fail to think fast when surrounded by the enemy is to have your back pressed to the wall; And to fail to take the battle to the enemy when your back is to the wall is to perish."

"In all fighting, the direct methods may be used for joining battle, but indirect methods will be needed in order to secure victory."

"Hence the saying: If you know the enemy and know yourself, you need not fear the result of a hundred battles. If you know yourself but not the enemy, for every victory gained you will also suffer a defeat. If you know neither the enemy nor yourself, you will succumb in every battle."

"Now, when your weapons are dulled, your ardor damped, your strength exhausted and your treasure spent, other chieftains will spring up to take advantage of your extremity. Then no man, however wise, will be able to avert the consequences that must ensue."

"In war, numbers alone confer no advantage."

"What is of the greatest importance in war is extraordinary speed: One cannot afford to neglect opportunity."

"The expert at battle seeks his victory from strategic advantage and does not demand it from his men. He is thus able to select the right men and exploit the strategic advantage. He who exploits the strategic advantage sends his men into battle like rolling logs and boulders. It is the nature of logs and boulders that on flat ground, they are stationary, but on steep ground, they roll; the square in shape tends to stop but the round tends to roll. Thus, that the strategic advantage of the expert commander in exploiting his men in battle can be likened to rolling round boulders down a steep ravine thousands of feet high says something about his strategic advantage."

## Morihei Ueshiba

"The more power the opponent uses, the easier it is for you... It's not that I am so strong; they were wrestling with themselves, and spending their energy on the air." The founder of Aikido, Morihei Ueshiba to one of his students.

## Vegetius

"Know the character of the enemy and their principal officers; whether they be rash or cautious, enterprising or timid, whether they fight on principle or from chance."

"The main and principal point in war is to secure plenty of provisions for oneself and to destroy the enemy by famine. Famine is more terrible than the sword."

## Sam Walton

"To succeed in this world, you have to change all the time."

"The airplane turned into a great tool for scouting real estate. From up in the air we could check out traffic flows, see which way cities and towns were growing, and evaluate the location of the competition – if there was any. Then we would develop our real estate strategy for that market... I'd get down low, turn my plane up on its side, and fly right over a town. Once we had a spot picked out, we'd land, go find out who owned the property, and try to negotiate the deal right then. That's another good reason I don't like jets. You can't get down low enough to really tell what's going on, the way I could in my little planes."

## George Washington

"Experience teaches us that it is much easier to prevent an enemy from posting themselves than it is to dislodge them after they have got possession."

## Thomas J. Watson

"If you want to be successful faster, you must double the rate of failure. Success lies on the far side of failure".
– Thomas J. Watson, the founder of IBM, when asked how one could succeed faster.

## Jack Welch

"...our whole thrust here was to get into the right businesses, find businesses with growth, get an organization that could respond to change quickly, and get as much out of the capital we employed as we possibly could... You look at some companies that have had more difficulties, they've been investing a lot of capital without getting much out of it. So using capital efficiently is clearly a driving force."

"If you don't have a competitive advantage, don't compete."

> "It is better to act too quickly than it is to wait too long."
>
> – Jack Welch

### John "Jocko" Willink

"Our freedom to operate and maneuver had increased substantially through disciplined procedures. Discipline equals freedom."

### John Wooden

"The best teacher is repetition day after day, throughout the season. I never gave my teams any kind of a written test. After all, they didn't have time in a game to sit down and write something. It had to be instant recognition and instant reaction."

"Over the years I have become convinced that every detail is important and that success usually accompanies attention to little details. It is this, in my judgment, that makes for the difference between champion and near-champion."

"In game play it was always my philosophy that patience would win out. By that, I meant patience to follow our game plan. If we believed in it, we would wear the opposition down and would eventually get to them. If we broke away from our style, however, and played their style, we would be in trouble. And if we let our emotions, rather than our reason, command the game we would not function effectively."

## Wu Qi

"If they [the enemy] are found to be in chaos, do not hesitate to attack them."

## Xenophon

"Here, too, is a maxim to engrave upon the memory: in charging a superior force, never to leave a difficult tract of ground in the rear of your attack, since there is all the difference in the world between a stumble in flight and a stumble in pursuit."

"Let us get rid of all inessentials in the rest of our equipment."

## Tsunetomo Yamamoto

"It's a difficult thing to truly know your own limits and points of weakness."

– From Hagakure: The Book of the Samurai. Hagagure was written by Tsunetomo Yamamoto. Hagakure, translated from Japanese as "Hidden by the Leaves" or "Hidden Leaves or "In the Shadow of Leaves", is a distillation of the code of Samurai Bushido (Warrior). This guide for the Samurai warrior was created from a compilation of discourses by the clerk Yamamoto Tsunetomo who served the powerful feudal lord Nabeshima Mitsushige during the early 1700's.

*Frederick II of Prussia*

# CHAPTER SEVEN

## On Innovation

"If you want something new, you have to stop doing something old."

– Peter F. Drucker

## Dhirubhai Ambani

"Play on the frontiers of technology. Be ahead of the tomorrows."

## Warren G. Bennis

"In life, change is inevitable. In business, change is vital."

## Max De Pree

"In the end, it is important to remember that we cannot become what we need to be, by remaining what we are."

## Peter Drucker

"People in any organization are always attached to the obsolete – the things that should have worked but did not, the things that once were productive and no longer are."

"Don't try to innovate for the future. Innovate for the present!"

## Larry Ellison

"When you innovate, you've got to be prepared for

everyone telling you you're nuts."

"When you are the first person whose beliefs are different from what everyone else believes, you are basically saying, 'I'm right and everyone else is wrong.' That's a very unpleasant position to be in. It's at once exhilaration and the same time an invitation to be attacked."

## Benjamin Franklin

"When you are finished changing, you're finished."

> "The greatest and noblest pleasure which men can have in this world is to discover new truths; and the next is to shake off old prejudices."
>
> – Frederick II

**Henry Ford**

"Few people dare get into business because, deep down, they say to themselves: 'Why should I put such and such a product on the market when somebody else is producing it already?' As for me, I've always said: 'Why not do better?' And that's what I did."

**Grace Murray Hopper**

The most damaging phrase in the language is "We've always done it this way!"

**Tony Hsieh**

"We must never lose our sense of urgency in making improvements. We must never settle for "good enough," because good is the enemy of great."

"So there are no experts in what we're doing. Except for us: we are becoming experts as we do this. And for anyone we bring on board, the best expertise they can bring is expertise at learning and adapting and figuring new things out – helping the company grow, and in the process they will also be growing themselves."

"We must all learn not only to not fear change, but to embrace it enthusiastically and, perhaps even more important, encourage and drive it."

**Steve Jobs**

"Innovation distinguishes between a leader and a follower."

"You have to be burning with an idea, or a problem, or a wrong that you want to right. If you're not passionate enough from the start, you'll never stick it out."

"People think focus means saying yes to the thing you've got to focus on. But that's not what it means at all. It means saying no to the hundred other good ideas that there are. You have to pick carefully. I'm actually as proud of the things we haven't done as the things I have done. Innovation is saying no to 1,000 things."

"If you just sit and observe, you will see how restless your mind is. If you try to calm it, it only makes it worse, but over time it does calm, and when it does, there's room to hear more subtle things – that's when your intuition starts to blossom and you start to see things more clearly and be in the present more. Your mind just slows down, and you see a tremendous expanse in the moment. You see so much more than you could see before. It's a discipline; you have to practice it."
– Walter Isaacson, from the biography,"

"Simple can be harder than complex: You have to work hard to get your thinking clean to make it simple. But it's worth it in the end because once you get there, you can move mountains."

"Taking LSD was a profound experience, one of the most important things in my life. LSD shows you that there's another side to the coin, and you can't remember it when it wears off, but you know it. It reinforced my sense of what was important – creating great things instead of making money, putting things back into the stream of history and of human consciousness as much as I could."

## Herb Kelleher

"You must be very patient, very persistent. The world isn't going to shower gold coins on you just because you have a good idea. You're going to have to work like crazy to bring that idea to the attention of people."

## Jack Ma

"I'm not a tech guy. I'm looking at the technology with the eyes of my customers, normal people's eyes."

## Niccolò Machiavelli

"A man who is used to acting in one way never changes; he must come to ruin when the times, in changing, no longer are in harmony with his ways."

'It must be considered that there is nothing more difficult to carry out, nor more doubtful of success, nor more dangerous to handle, than to initiate a new order of things. For the reformer has enemies in all those who profit by the old order, and only lukewarm defenders in all those who would profit by the new order, this lukewarmness arising partly from fear of their adversaries, who have the laws in their favor; and partly from the incredulity of mankind, who do not truly believe in anything new until they have had the actual experience of it."

## Richard "Dick" Marcinko

"Change hurts. It makes people insecure, confused, and angry. People want things to be the same as they've always been, because that makes life easier. But, if you're a leader, you can't let your people hang on to the past."

## Albert Szent-Györgyi de Nagyrápolt

"Discovery consists of seeing what everybody has seen and thinking what nobody has thought."

## Napoleon I

"Ten people who speak make more noise than ten thousand who are silent."

"Imagination governs the world."

## Larry Page

"Lots of companies don't succeed over time. What do they fundamentally do wrong? They usually miss the future. I try to focus on that: What is the future really going to be? And how do we create it? And how do we power our organization to really focus on that and really drive it at a high rate?"

"Invention is not enough. Tesla invented the electric power we use, but he struggled to get it out to people. You have to combine both things: invention and innovation focus, plus the company that can commercialize things and get them to people."

## Hyman G. Rickover

"When I came to Washington before World War II to head the electrical section of the Bureau of Ships, I found that one man was in charge of design, another of production, a third handled maintenance, while a fourth dealt with fiscal matters. The entire bureau operated that way. It didn't make sense to me. Design problems showed up in production, production errors showed up in maintenance, and financial matters reached into all areas. I changed the system. I made one man responsible for his entire area of equipment – for design, production, maintenance, and contracting. If anything went wrong, I knew exactly at whom to point. I run my present organization on the same principle."

## Jack Welch

"If the rate of change on the outside exceeds the rate of change on the inside, the end is near."

"When launching something new, you have to go for it – 'playing not to lose' can never be an option."

## Robert Anton Wilson

"Every fact of science was once damned. Every invention was considered impossible. Every discovery was a nervous shock to some orthodoxy. Every artistic innovation was denounced as fraud and folly. The entire web of culture and 'progress', everything on earth that is man-made and not given to us by nature, is the concrete manifestation of some man's refusal to bow to Authority. We would own no more, know no more, and be no more than the first apelike hominids if it were not for the rebellious, the recalcitrant, and the intransigent. As Oscar Wilde truly said, 'Disobedience was man's Original Virtue.'"

## John Wooden

"If you're not making mistakes, then you're not doing anything. I'm positive that a doer makes mistakes."

## Leonardo da Vinci

"The men of experiment are like the ant; they only collect and use. But the bee gathers its materials from the flowers of the garden and of the field, but transforms and digests it by a power of its own."

# CHAPTER EIGHT

## Ethical Challenges of Leadership

"A person may cause evil to others not only by his actions but by his inaction, and in either case he is justly accountable to them for the injury."

– John Stuart Mill

## Marcus Aurelius

"Only attend to thyself, and resolve to be a good man in every act which thou dost."

"The object of life is not to be on the side of the majority, but to escape finding oneself in the ranks of the insane."

"Do not be whirled about, but in every movement have respect to justice."

## Richard Branson

"There have been times when I could have succumbed to some form of bribe, or could have had my way by offering one. But ever since that night in Dover prison I have never been tempted to break my vow... My parents always drummed into me that all you have in life is your reputation: you may be very rich, but if you lose your good name you'll never be happy."

## Edmund Burke

"When bad men combine, the good must associate; else they will fall one by one, an unpitied sacrifice in a contemptible struggle."

## James MacGregor Burns

"Divorced from ethics, leadership is reduced to management and politics to mere technique."

## Julius Caesar

"All bad precedents begin as justifiable measures."

## Cicero

"What is morally wrong can never be advantageous, even when it enables you to make some gain that you believe to be to your advantage. The mere act of believing that some wrongful course of action constitutes an advantage is pernicious."

"Diseases of the soul are more dangerous and more numerous than those of the body."

"I conclude, then, that the plea of having acted in the interests of a friend is not a valid excuse for a wrong action. . . . We may then lay down this rule of friendship – neither ask nor consent to do what is wrong. For the plea "for friendship's sake" is a discreditable one, and not to be admitted for a moment."

## Roy E. Disney

"When your values are clear to you, making decisions becomes easier."

## Peter Drucker

"Management is doing things right; leadership is doing the right things."

## Queen Elizabeth I

"A clear and innocent conscience fears nothing."

## Mary Parker Follett

"One of the primary ways leaders contribute to an unethical and potentially corrupt organization is by failing to speak up, against acts they believe are wrong. A leader who holds his tongue in order to fit in is essentially giving his or her support for unethical behavior. If a leader knows someone is being treated unfairly by a colleague and does nothing, the leader is setting a precedent to others to behave unfairly as well. Peers and subordinates with lax ethical standards often feel free to act as they choose. It is often hard to stand up for what is right, but this is a primary way in which leaders create an environment of integrity."

## Mahatma Gandhi

"Silence becomes cowardice when occasion demands speaking out the whole truth and acting accordingly."

"There are seven things that will destroy us: Wealth without work; Pleasure without conscience; Knowledge without character; Religion without sacrifice; Politics without principle; Science without humanity; Business without ethics."

> "To believe in something, and not to live it, is dishonest."
>
> – Mahatma Gandhi

"Manliness consists not in bluff, bravado or loneliness. It consists in daring to do the right thing and facing consequences whether it is in matters social, political or other. It consists in deeds not words."

"A 'No' uttered from the deepest conviction is better than a 'Yes' merely uttered to please, or worse, to avoid trouble."

## Baltasar Gracián

"Never open the door to a lesser evil, for other and greater ones invariably slink in after it."

## Patrick Henry

"The eternal difference between right and wrong does not fluctuate, it is immutable."

"We are apt to shut our eyes against a painful truth... For my part, I am willing to know the whole truth; to know the worst; and to provide for it."

"We lie the loudest when we lie to ourselves."

– Eric Hoffer

## Thomas Jefferson

"He who permits himself to tell a lie once, finds it much easier to do it the second time."

"When injustice becomes law, resistance becomes duty."

"There is a debt of service due from every man to his country, proportioned to the bounties which nature & fortune have measured to him."
– Thomas Jefferson in a letter to Edward Rutledge, December 27th, 1796.

## Lyndon Johnson

"Doing what is right isn't the problem. It is knowing what is right."

## John F. Kennedy

"A man does what he must... in spite of personal consequences, in spite of obstacles and dangers, and pressures... and that is the basis of all human morality."

## Robert F. Kennedy

"Few men are willing to brave the disapproval of their fellows, the censure of their colleagues, the wrath of their society. Moral courage is a rarer commodity than bravery in battle or great intelligence. Yet it is the one essential, vital quality for those who seek to change a world which yields most painfully to change."

## Martin Luther King Jr.

"The ultimate measure of a man is not where he stands in moments of comfort, but where he stands at times of challenge and controversy."

## Abraham Lincoln

"If there is anything that links the human to the divine, it is the courage to stand by a principle when everybody else rejects it."

"The probability that we might fail in the struggle ought not to deter us from the support of a cause we believe to be just."

"Be with a leader when he is right, stay with him when he is still right, but, leave him when he is wrong."

"No man has a good enough memory to be a successful liar."

## Douglas MacArthur

"No nation can safely trust its martial honor to leaders who do not maintain the universal code which distinguishes between those things that are right and those things that are wrong."

"Last, but by no means least, courage of one's convictions, the courage to see things through. The world is in a constant conspiracy against the brave. It's the age-old struggle: the roar of the crowd on one side and the voice of your conscience on the other."

## Niccolò Machiavelli

"Any man who tries to be good all the time is bound to come to ruin among the great number who are not good. Hence a prince who wants to keep his authority must learn how not to be good, and use that knowledge, or refrain from using it, as necessity requires."

> "The language of truth is unadorned and always simple."
>
> – Ammianus Marcellinus

## Elon Musk

"I need to be protected against a private equity firm or hedge fund trying to force me to maximize profitability rather than affecting the future of humanity in a positive way. That's why I have to have a controlling stake, or close to one, in all of my ventures."

## Napoleon I

"This soldier, I realized, must have had friends at home and in his regiment; yet he lay there deserted by all except his dog. I looked on, unmoved, at battles which decided the future of nations. Tearless, I had given orders which brought death to thousands. Yet here I was stirred, profoundly stirred, stirred to tears. And by what? By the grief of one dog."

## George S. Patton Jr.

"Moral courage is the most valuable and usually the most absent characteristic in men."

## H. Ross Perot

"You will need a great deal of self-discipline not to lose your sense of balance, humility, and commitment."

## Hyman G. Rickover

"I believe it is the duty of each of us to act as if the fate of the world depended on him. Admittedly, one man by himself cannot do the job. However, one man can make a difference. We must live for the future of the human race, and not for our own comfort or success."

## Eleanor Roosevelt

"Do what you feel in your heart to be right, for you'll be criticized anyway."

## Theodore Roosevelt

"There is a point, of course, where a man must take the isolated peak and break with it all for clear principle, but until it comes he must work, if he would be of use, with men as they are. As long as the good in them overbalances the evil, let him work with that for the best that can be got."

## Sallust

"No mortal man has ever served at the same time his passions and his best interests."

## Norman Schwarzkopf

"The truth of the matter is that you always know the right thing to do. The hard part is doing it."

## James Stockdale

"I think character is permanent, and issues are transient."

"One final aspect of leadership is the frequent necessity to be a philosopher, able to understand and to explain the lack of a moral economy in this universe, for many people have a great deal of difficulty with the fact that virtue is not always rewarded nor is evil always punished. To handle tragedy may indeed be the mark of an educated man, for one of the principal goals of education is to prepare us for failure. To say that is not to encourage resignation to the whims of fate, but to acknowledge the need for forethought about how to cope with undeserved reverses. It's important that our leadership steel themselves against the natural reaction of lashing out or withdrawing when it happens. The test of character is not 'hanging in there' when the light at the end of the tunnel is expected but performance of duty and persistence of example when the situation rules out the possibility of the light ever coming."

## Sun Bin

"Commanders must have integrity; without integrity, they have no power. If they have no power, they cannot bring out the best in their armies. Therefore, integrity is the hand of warriorship."

## George Washington

"Few men have virtue to withstand the highest bidder."

"Still I hope I shall always possess firmness and virtue enough to maintain (what I consider the most enviable of all titles) the character of an honest man."
– George Washington in a letter to Alexander Hamilton, Thursday, August 28, 1788.

"Labor to keep alive in your breast that little spark of celestial fire called conscience."
– George Washington, Rules of Civility And Other Writings & Speeches.

## John Wooden

"Ethics and Attitude. Be more concerned with your character than with your reputation. Character is what you really are. Reputation is what people say you are. Character is more important."

*Ulysses S. Grant*

# CHAPTER NINE

## On Organizational Leadership

"There is nothing quite so useless as doing with great efficiency something that should not be done at all."

– Peter F. Drucker

## Chanakya, The Indian Machiavelli

"A person with (theoretical) knowledge, but without practical experience, comes to grief in the accomplishment of tasks."

## Winston S. Churchill

"If you have an important point to make, don't try to be subtle or clever. Use a pile driver. Hit the point once. Then come back and hit it again. Then hit it a third time – a tremendous whack."

## W. Edwards Deming

"Learning is not compulsory... neither is survival."

"If you can't describe what you are doing as a process, you don't know what you're doing."

## Max De Pree

"The signs of outstanding leadership appear primarily among the followers. Are the followers reaching their potential? Are they learning? Serving? Do they achieve the required results? Do they change with grace? Manage conflict?"

## Peter Drucker

"So much of what we call management consists in making it difficult for people to work."

## Ludwig Wilhelm Erhard

"A compromise is the art of dividing a cake in such a way that everyone believes he has the biggest piece."

## Clarence Francis

"You can buy a man's time, you can buy a man's physical presence at a certain place, you can even buy a measured number of skilled muscular motions per hour or day. But you cannot buy enthusiasm, you cannot buy initiative, you cannot buy loyalty; you cannot buy the devotion of hearts, minds, and souls. You have to earn these things."

## Bill Gates

"Give your workers more sophisticated jobs along with better tools, and you'll discover that your employees will become more responsible and bring more intelligence to their work. One-dimensional, repetitive work is exactly what computers, robots and other machines are best at – and what human workers are poorly suited to and almost uniformly despise. In the digital age, you need to make knowledge workers out of every employee possible."

## Genghis Khan

"Conquering the world on horseback is easy; it is dismounting and governing that is hard."

## Jim Goodnight

"Treat employees like they make a difference and they will."

## Ulysses S. Grant

"Two commanders on the same field are always one too many."

"The distant rear of an army engaged in battle is not the best place from which to judge correctly what is going on in front."

## Dee Hock

"The essence of community, its heart and soul, is the non-monetary exchange of value; things we do and share because we care for others, and for the good of the place."

## Jiang Taigong

"In a major campaign, everyone should be trained to use the equipment."

> "Talent wins games, but teamwork and intelligence wins championships."
>
> – Michael Jordan

## Vince Lombardi Jr.

"You have to start by teaching the fundamentals. A player's got to know the basics of the game and how to play his position. Next, you've got to keep him in line. That's discipline. The men have to play as a team, not as a bunch of individuals. There's no room for prima donnas. Then you come to the third ingredient: if you're going to play together as a team, you've got to care for one another. You've got to love each other. Each player has to be thinking of the other guy and saying to himself: If I don't block that man, Paul is going to get his legs broken I have to do my job well in order that he can do his."

**Harvey MacKay**

"Don't equate activity with efficiency. You are paying your key people to see the big picture. Don't let them get bogged down in a lot of meaningless meetings and paper shuffling. Announce a Friday afternoon off once in a while. Cancel a Monday morning meeting or two. Tell the cast of characters you'd like them to spend the amount of time normally spent preparing for attending the meeting at their desks, simply thinking about an original idea."

**Bernard Law Montgomery**

"Every soldier must know, before he goes into battle, how the little battle he is to fight fits into the larger picture, and how the success of his fighting will influence the battle as a whole."

**Napoleon I**

"When I give a minister an order, I leave it to him to find the means to carry it out."

"One should never forbid what one lacks the power to prevent."

## Charlton Ogburn

"We trained hard, but it seemed that every time we were beginning to form up into teams we would be reorganized. Presumably the plans for our employment were being changed. I was to learn later in life that, perhaps because we are so good at organizing, we tend as a nation to meet any new situation by reorganizing; and a wonderful method it can be for creating the illusion of progress while producing confusion, inefficiency, and demoralization."

– Charlton Ogburn, "Merrill's Marauders, the truth about an incredible adventure," Harper's Magazine, January 1957.

## Larry Page

"We don't have as many managers as we should, but we would rather have too few than too many."

## Theodore Roosevelt

"The best executive is the one who has sense enough to pick good men to do what he wants done, and self-restraint enough to keep from meddling with them while they do it."

> "Example is leadership."
>
> – Albert Schweitzer

## Thucydides

"It is frequently a misfortune to have very brilliant men in charge of affairs. They expect too much of ordinary men."

## Brian Urquhart

"Don't ask either party to commit suicide. Provide a graceful way out."
– Former United Nations Undersecretary General Brian Urquhart, from comments at a seminar on the United Nations sponsored by the Aspen Institute for Humanistic Studies, Wye Plantation, Maryland, December 4th, 1982.

## John "Jocko" Willink

"In any team, in any organization, all responsibility for

success and failure rests with the leader. The leader must own everything in his or her world. There is no one else to blame. The leader must acknowledge mistakes and admit failures, take ownership of them, and develop a plan to win."

## John Wooden

"Our emphasis is on teaching the quick and proper execution of the fundamentals."

"Don't mistake activity for achievement. To produce results, tasks must be well organized and properly executed; otherwise, it's no different from children running around the playground – everybody is doing something, but nothing is being done; lots of activity, no achievement."

"The best teacher is repetition day after day, throughout the season. I never gave my teams any kind of a written test. After all, they didn't have time in a game to sit down and write something. It had to be instant recognition and instant reaction."

## Jack Welch

If you pick the right people and give them the opportunity to spread their wings and put compensation as a carrier behind it you almost don't have to manage them."

## Xenophon

"One day when Socrates met a man who had been chosen general, he asked him, "For what reason, think you, is Agamemnon dubbed 'Shepherd of the people' by Homer? Is it because a shepherd must see that his sheep are safe and are fed, and that the object for which they are kept is attained, and a general must see that his men are safe and are fed, and that the object for which they fight is attained, or, in other words, that victory over the enemy may add to their happiness? Or what reason can Homer have for praising Agamemnon as "both a good king and a brave warrior" too? Is it that he would be 'a brave warrior too' not if he alone were a good fighter, but if he made all his men like himself; and 'a good king' not if he merely ordered his own life aright, but if he made his subjects happy as well? Because a king is chosen, not to take good care of himself, but for the good of those who have chosen him; and all men fight in order that they may get the best life possible, and choose generals to guide them to it. Therefore it is the duty of a commander to contrive this for those who have chosen him for general. For anything more honorable than that is not easy to find, or anything more disgraceful than its opposite." By these reflections on what constitutes a good leader he stripped away all other virtues, and left just the power to make his followers happy.
– Xenophon, Socratic Memoirs 3.2.1-3.

# CHAPTER TEN

## On Being a New Leader

"More leaders have been made by accident, circumstance, sheer grit, or will than have been made by all the leadership courses put together."

– Warren Bennis

## Warren Bennis

"The most dangerous leadership myth is that leaders are born – that there is a genetic factor to leadership. This myth asserts that people simply either have certain charismatic qualities or not. That's nonsense; in fact, the opposite is true. Leaders are made rather than born."

"The manager accepts the status quo; the leader challenges it."

## Richard Branson

"Listen – it makes you sound smarter"

## Winston S. Churchill

"To each there comes in their lifetime a special moment when they are figuratively tapped on the shoulder and offered the chance to do a very special thing, unique to them and fitted to their talents. What a tragedy if that moment finds them unprepared or unqualified for that which could have been their finest hour."

"The price of greatness is responsibility."

## Peter Drucker

"Your first and foremost job as a leader is to take charge of your own energy and then help to orchestrate the energy of those around you."

## Dwight D. Eisenhower

"As a final word, he said, let me offer one item of advice. It is that you must be tough. You must be tough with your immediate commanders and they must be equally tough with their respective subordinates. We have passed the time where we cannot demand from troops reasonable results after you have made careful plans and preparations and estimated that the task can be accomplished..."

## Queen Elizabeth I

"To be a king and wear a crown is more glorious to them that see it than it is a pleasure to bear it."

## Benjamin Franklin

"Being ignorant is not so much a shame, as being unwilling to learn."

## Harold Geneen

"In the business world, everyone is paid in two coins: cash and experience. Take the experience first; the cash will come later."

## Baltasar Gracián

"Do not enter where too much is anticipated. It is the misfortune of the over-celebrated that they cannot measure up to excessive expectations. The actual can never attain the imagined: for to think perfection is easy, but to embody it is most difficult. The imagination weds the wish, and together they always conjure up more than reality can furnish. For however great may be a person's virtues, the will never measure up to what was imagined. When people see themselves cheated in their extravagant anticipations, they turn more quickly to disparagement than to praise. Hope is a great falsifier of the truth; the intelligence put her right by seeing to it that the fruit is superior to its appetite. You will make a better exit when the actual transcends the imagined, and is more than was expected."

## Vince Lombardi Jr.

"Leaders aren't born, they are made. And they are made just like anything else, through hard work. And that's the price we'll have to pay to achieve that goal, or any goal."

*Baltasar Gracián*

## Douglas MacArthur

"A true leader has the confidence to stand alone, the courage to make tough decisions, and the compassion to listen to the needs of others. He does not set out to be a leader, but becomes one by the equality of his actions and the integrity of his intent."

## Niccolò Machiavelli

"It must be considered that there is nothing more difficult to carry out, nor more doubtful of success, nor more dangerous to handle, than to initiate a new order of things. For the reformer has enemies in all those who profit by the old order, and only lukewarm defenders in all those who would profit by the new order, this lukewarmness arising partly from fear of their adversaries, who have the laws in their favor; and partly from the incredulity of mankind, who do not truly believe in anything new until they have had the actual experience of it."

## Bernard Montgomery

"The first thing a young officer must do when he joins the Army is to fight a battle, and that battle is for the hearts of his men. If he wins that battle and subsequent similar ones, his men will follow him anywhere; if he loses it, he will never do any real good."

## Mother Teresa

"Do not wait for leaders; do it alone, person to person."

## Loretta "Lori" Reynolds

"Anytime you're going to take your Marines into harm's

way, they are looking for leadership that is calm, assertive, sure of themselves. And quite honestly, I don't think that some of these young Marines care if it's a male or a female. They just want to be properly led."

## Antoine de Saint-Exupery

"A chief is a man who assumes responsibility. He says 'I was beaten', he does not say 'My men were beaten.'"

## Norman Schwarzkopf

"When placed in command, take charge."

## James Stockdale

"Great leaders gain authority by giving it away."

## George Washington

"But lest some unlucky event should happen unfavorable to my reputation, I beg it may be remembered by every gentleman in the room that I this day declare with the utmost sincerity, I do not think myself equal to the command I am honored with."

*Franklin D. Roosevelt*

# CHAPTER ELEVEN

## On Becoming a Visionary

"...If one advances confidently in the direction of his dreams, and endeavors to live the life which he has imagined, he will meet with a success unexpected in common hours... If you have built castles in the air, your work need not be lost; that is where they should be. Now put the foundations under them."

– Henry David Thoreau

## Dhirubhai Ambani

"Secret of my success was to have ambition and know minds of men."

## Marcus Aurelius

"Look back over the past, with its changing empires that rose and fell, and you can foresee the future too."

## Bernard M. Baruch

"Millions saw the apple fall, but Newton was the one who asked why."

## Warren Bennis

"Leadership is the capacity to translate vision into reality."

## Richard Branson

"All ideas are second-hand, consciously or unconsciously drawn from a million outside sources, and daily used by the garnerer with a pride and satisfaction born of the superstition that he originated them."

## Winston S. Churchill

"The farther backward you can look, the farther forward you are likely to see."

## Larry Ellison

"The most important aspect of my personality as far as determining my success goes, has been my questioning conventional wisdom, doubting experts and questioning authority. While that can be painful in your relationships with your parents and teachers, it's enormously useful in life."

"The only way to get ahead is to find errors in conventional wisdom."

## John Kenneth Galbraith

"All of the great leaders have had one characteristic in common: it was the willingness to confront unequivocally the major anxiety of their people in their time. This, and not much else, is the essence of leadership".

## Thomas Jefferson

"I like the dreams of the future better than the history of the past."

## Robert F. Kennedy

"Only those who dare to fail greatly can ever achieve greatly."

"Some people see things as they are and say: why? I dream things that never were and say: why not?"
– Robert F. Kennedy borrowing from George Bernard Shaw.

"All men dream: but not equally. Those who dream by night in the dusty recesses of their minds wake up in the day to find it was vanity, but the dreamers of the day are dangerous men, for they may act their dreams with open eyes, to make it possible."

– T. E. Lawrence (Lawrence of Arabia)

## Abraham Lincoln

"Towering genius disdains a beaten path. It seeks regions unexplored."

## Niccolò Machiavelli

"To know in war how to recognize an opportunity and seize it is better than anything else."

## J. P. Morgan

"Go as far as you can see; when you get there, you'll be able to see farther."

## Miyamoto Musashi

"From one thing, know ten thousand things"

– Miyamoto Musashi, The Book of Five Rings

## Hyman Rickover

"Good ideas are not adopted automatically. They must be driven into practice with courageous patience."

## Francois duc de La Rochefoucauld

"Those who spend their time on small things usually become incapable of large ones."

## Franklin D. Roosevelt

"The country needs and, unless I mistake its temper, the country demands bold, persistent experimentation. It is common sense to take a method and try it: If it fails, admit it frankly and try another. But above all, try something."
– Franklin D. Roosevelt, Address at Oglethorpe University, May 22, 1932.

## Carl Schurz

"Ideals are like stars; you will not succeed in touching them with your hands. But like the seafaring man on the desert of waters, you choose them as your guides, and following them you will reach your destiny."

## Takeda Shingen

"A man with deep far-sightedness will survey both the beginning and the end of a situation and continually consider its every facet as important."

**Harry S. Truman**

"How far would Moses have gone if had taken a poll in Egypt?"

**Jack Welch**

"Good business leaders create a vision, articulate the vision, passionately own the vision, and relentlessly drive it to completion."

"Change before you have to."

# PART TWO
# LEADERS & FOLLOWERS

*Heraclitus, as painted by Johannes Moreelse*

# CHAPTER TWELVE

## On Building Your Team

"Great things in business are never done by one person. They're done by a team of people."

– Steve Jobs

## Warren G. Bennis

"Too many companies believe people are interchangeable. Truly gifted people never are. They have unique talents. Such people cannot be forced into roles they are not suited for, nor should they be. Effective leaders allow great people to do the work they were born to do."

## Otto von Bismarck

"The right people in the right jobs."

## Richard Branson

"Train people well enough so they can leave. Treat them well enough so they don't want to."

## Julius Caesar

"Without training, they lacked knowledge. Without knowledge, they lacked confidence. Without confidence, they lacked victory."

"It is easier to find men who will volunteer to die, than to find those who are willing to endure pain with patience."

## Chanakya, The Indian Machiavelli

"Training can impart discipline to those who are suitable material, not to those who are not."

"Classmates, though they are trustworthy, will not respect the ruler, having been playmates. Hence they should not be appointed as ministers."

"From the skill exhibited in performance is a man's capacity assessed."

"What character the ruler has, the people attendant on him have."

"A learned scholar without world experience, is equal to a fool."

## Peter Drucker

"No institution can possibly survive if it needs geniuses or supermen to manage it. It must be organized in such a way as to be able to get along under a leadership composed of average human beings."

"The better a man is the more mistakes he will make, for the more new things he will try. I would never promote to a top-level a man who was not making mistakes otherwise I am sure he is a mediocre."

**Bill Gates**

"As we look ahead into the next century, leaders will be those who empower others."

**Heraclitus**

"Out of every one hundred men, ten shouldn't even be there, eighty are just targets, nine are the real fighters, and we are lucky to have them, for they make the battle. Ah, but the one, one is a warrior, and he will bring the others back."

**Special Forces/Delta Operator MSG Paul R. Howe**

"Generally, success or failure of the mission can be tracked down to a leadership void in the selection or training of the personnel at the individual, team or organizational level of the tactical element."

**Herb Kelleher**

"We will hire someone with less experience, less education, and less expertise, than someone who has more of those things and has a rotten attitude. Because we can train people. We can teach people how to lead. We can teach people how to provide customer service. But we can't change their DNA."

"I forgive all personal weaknesses except egomania and pretension."

"You don't hire for skills, you hire for attitude. You can always teach skills."

**Vince Lombardi Jr.**

"The will to win is not nearly as important as the will to prepare to win."

"The first method for estimating the intelligence of a ruler is to look at the men he has around him."

– Niccolò Machiavelli

**Harvey MacKay**

"Don't water your weeds."

## Elon Musk

"As much as possible, avoid hiring MBA's. MBA programs don't teach people how to create companies."

## Netflix internal "Culture Deck"

"Which of my people, if they told me they were leaving for a similar job at a competitor or peer company would I fight hard to keep?"
– "The Keeper Test" From Netflix internal "culture deck" articulating their company culture and expectations.

## Napoleon I

"The first virtue of a soldier is endurance of fatigue; courage is only the second virtue."

## Ronald Reagan

"Surround yourself with great people; delegate authority; get out of the way."

## Franklin D. Roosevelt

"I'm not the smartest fellow in the world, but I can sure pick smart colleagues."

"If in the darkness of ignorance, you don't recognize a person's true nature, look to see whom he has chosen for his leader."

– Rumi

## U.S. Army Special Operations

"Selection is a never ending process."
– U.S. Army Special Operations maxim.

## Sun Tzu

"The man who was ready to 'beard a tiger or rush a river' without caring whether he lived or died – that sort of man I should not take. I should certainly take someone who approached difficulties with due caution and who preferred to succeed by strategy."

– Sun Tzu, author of The Art of War, responding to Tzu Lu, a disciple of Confucius, when asked who he would take into battle with him.

## Sam Walton

"If you take someone who lacks the experience and the know-how but has the real desire and the willingness to work his tail off to get the job done, he'll make up for what he lacks. And that proved true nine times out of ten."

## George Washington

"It is infinitely better to have a few good men than many indifferent ones."
– George Washington in a letter to James McHenry, Friday, August 10, 1798.

"Discipline is the soul of an army. It makes small numbers formidable; procures success to the weak, and esteem to all."

## Jack Welch

On hiring: "I want somebody with incredible energy who can excite others, who can define their vision, who finds change fun and doesn't get paralyzed by it. I want somebody who feels comfortable in Delhi or Denver. I mean, somebody who really feels comfortable and can talk to all kinds of people. I don't know what the world's going to be; all I know is it's going to be nothing like it is today. It's going to be faster; information's going to be everywhere."

## John "Jocko" Willink

"After all, there can be no leadership where there is no team."

## Wu Qi

"One man who has been trained in warfare can instruct ten men. Ten men who have been trained can train a hundred men. A hundred men who have been trained can train a thousand men. A thousand men who have been trained can train ten thousand men. Ten thousand men who have been trained can train the whole army."

## Xenophon

"It follows, therefore, as a matter of course, that he who devotes himself to a very specialized line of work is bound to do it in the best possible manner."

*Alexander the Great, as envisioned by Jean-Simon Berthélemy*

# CHAPTER THIRTEEN

## On Creating Company Culture

"The culture of any organization is shaped by the worst behavior the leader is willing to tolerate."

– Steve Gruenert and Todd Whitaker

**Marcus Aurelius**

"Teach them then, and show them without being angry."

> "Remember, upon the conduct of each depends the fate of all."
>
> – Alexander the Great

**Mary Kay Ash**

"The speed of the leader is the speed of the gang."

**Leif Babin**

"It's not what you preach, it's what you tolerate."

**Warren G. Bennis**

"Trust is the lubrication that makes it possible for organizations to work."

## Richard Branson

"Clients do not come first. Employees come first. If you take care of your employees, they will take care of the clients."

## James MacGregor Burns

"In real life, the most practical advice for leaders is not to treat pawns like pawns, nor princes like princes, but all persons like persons."

## Catherine the Great

"One cannot always know what children are thinking. Children are hard to understand, especially when careful training has accustomed them to obedience, and experience has made them cautious in their conversation with their teachers. Will you not draw from this the fine maxim that one should not scold children too much, but should make them trustful, so that they will not conceal their stupidities from us?"

## Chanakya, The Indian Machiavelli

"No one should be disrespected. Everyone's opinion shall be heard. The wise one should utilize even a child's sensible words."

"A ruler with character can render even unendowed people happy. A characterless ruler destroys loyal and prosperous people."

"Inaccessible rulers destroy the people."

"If rulers are righteous, people are righteous, if they are sinners, people are also sinners; like ruler, like people."

## Winston S. Churchill

"When eagles are silent, parrots begin to chatter."

## Confucius

"There is never a case when the root is in disorder and yet the branches are in order."

## W. Edwards Deming

"The worker is not the problem. The problem is at the top! Management!"

> "A bad system will beat a good person every time."
>
> – W. Edwards Deming

## Peter Drucker

"The leaders who work most effectively, it seems to me, never say "I." And that's not because they have trained themselves not to say "I." They don't think "I." They think "we"; they think "team." They understand their job to be to make the team function. They accept responsibility and don't sidestep it, but "we" gets the credit. This is what creates trust, what enables you to get the task done."

## Dwight D. Eisenhower

"I have developed almost an obsession as to the certainty with which you can judge a division, or any other large unit, merely by knowing its commander intimately. Of course, we have had pounded into us all through our school courses that the exact level of a commander's personality and ability is always reflected in his unit – but

I did not realize, until opportunity came for comparisons on a rather large scale, how infallibly the commander and unit are almost one and the same thing."

**Larry Ellison**

"When I started Oracle, what I wanted to do was to create an environment where I would enjoy working. That was my primary goal. Sure, I wanted to make a living. I certainly never expected to become rich, certainly not this rich. I mean, rich does not even describe this. This is surreal. And it has nothing to do with money. I mean, you buy clothes with money, and cars. But I really wanted to work with people I enjoyed working with, who I admired and liked."

"Don't explain your philosophy. Embody it."

– Epictetus

## Harold S. Geneen

"No one wants to follow a weak leader. He is the worst kind. You cannot rely on his judgment because you don't know what he will do in a difficult situation. Much more respect and loyalty are given to the tough leader, the one who is not afraid to make to make difficult and even unpopular decisions, just as long as he is perceived to be decent and fair and reliable in his dealings with his subordinates."

## Genghis Khan

"I will rule them by fixed laws so that rest and happiness shall prevail in the world."
– Genghis Khan after being named Khan.

"Be of one mind and one faith, that you may conquer your enemies and lead long and happy lives."

## Grace Murray Hopper

"You manage things; you lead people."

## Tony Hsieh

"Your personal core values define who you are, and a company's core values ultimately define the company's character and brand. For individuals, character is destiny. For organizations, culture is destiny."

## Jiang Taigong

"If the general is not benevolent, then the army will not be close to or support him. If the general is not courageous, then the army will not be fierce. If the general is not wise, then the army will be in doubts. If the general is not perspicacious, then the army will be confounded. If the general is not quick-witted and acute, then the army will lose the opportunity. If the general is not constantly alert, the army will be weak in defense. If the general is not strong and forceful, then the army will fail in their duty. Thus the general is the Master of Fate. The army is ordered because of him, and they are disordered because of him as well. If one obtains someone who is worthy to serve as general, the army will be strong and the state will prosper. If one does not obtain a worthy as general, the army will be weak and state will perish."

## Steve Jobs

"Be a yardstick of quality. Some people aren't used to an environment where excellence is expected."

> "Men should be taught and won over by reason, not by blows, insults, and corporal punishments."
>
> – Julian the Apostate

## A. P. J. Abdul Kalam

"What makes life in... organizations difficult is the widespread prevalence of this very contemptuous pride. It stops us from listening to our juniors, subordinates and people down the line. You cannot expect a person to deliver results if you humiliate him, nor can you expect him to be creative if you abuse him or despise him. The line between firmness and harshness, between strong leadership and bullying, between discipline and vindictiveness is very fine, but it has to be drawn."

## Herb Kelleher

"A company is stronger if it is bound by love rather than by fear."

"One piece of advice that always stuck in my mind is that people should be respected and trusted as people, not because of their position or title."

"If you create an environment where the people truly participate, you don't need control. They know what needs to be done and they do it. And the more that people will devote themselves to your cause on a voluntary basis, a willing basis, the fewer hierarchies and control mechanisms you need."

## John F. Kennedy

"Conformity is the jailer of freedom and the enemy of growth."

## Bernard Montgomery

"The first thing a young officer must do when he joins the Army is to fight a battle, and that battle is for the hearts of his men. If he wins that battle and subsequent similar ones, his men will follow him anywhere; if he loses it, he will never do any real good."

*Field Marshal Bernard Law Montgomery*
*1st Viscount Montgomery of Alamein*

**Elon Musk**

"You can't only look at what an individual employee gets done. You also have to look at how they've helped people around them get things done."

**Audie Murphy**

"Loyalty to your comrades, when you come right down to it, has more to do with bravery in battle than even patriotism does. You may want to be brave, but your spirit can desert you when things really get rough. Only you find you can't let your comrades down and in the pinch they can't let you down either."

**Napoleon I**

"There is no authority without justice."

**George S. Patton**

"If you can't get them to salute when they should salute and wear the clothes you tell them to wear, how are you going to get them to die for their country?"

"Discipline can only be obtained when all officers are so imbued with the sense of their awful obligation to their men and to their country that they cannot tolerate negligence. Officers who fail to correct errors or to praise excellence are valueless in peace and dangerous misfits in war."

## H. Ross Perot

"Inventories can be managed, but people must be led."

"Widespread intellectual and moral docility may be convenient for leaders in the short term, but it is suicidal for nations and organizations in the long term. One of the criteria for national leadership should therefore be a talent for understanding, encouraging, and making constructive use of vigorous criticism."

– Carl Sagan

## Sam Walton

"I learned a long time ago that exercising your ego in public is definitely not the way to build an effective organization."

## Sun Tzu

"Regard your soldiers as your children, and they will follow you into the deepest valleys; look on them as your own beloved sons, and they will stand by you even unto death."

"When the men are punished before their loyalty is secured, they will be rebellious and disobedient. If disobedient and rebellious, it is difficult to deploy them. When the loyalty of the men is secured, but punishments are not enforced, such troops cannot be used either. Thus, the general must be able to instruct his troops with civility and humanity and unite them with rigorous training and discipline so as to secure victories in battles."

"Pay heed to nourishing the troops; do not unnecessarily fatigue them. Unite them in spirit; conserve their strength. Make unfathomable plans for the movement of the army. Thus, such troops need no encouragement to be vigilant. Without extorting their support the general obtains it; without inviting their affection he gains it; without demanding their trust he wins it."

"Soldiers must be treated in the first instance with humanity, but kept under control by means of iron discipline. This is a certain road to victory."

"When one treats people with benevolence, justice, and righteousness, and reposes confidence in them, the army will be united in mind and all will be happy to serve their leaders."

"If you are indulgent, but unable to make your authority felt; kind-hearted, but unable to enforce your commands; and incapable, moreover, of quelling disorder, your soldiers are like spoiled children: they are useless for any practical purpose."

## George Washington

"Discipline is the soul of an army. It makes small numbers formidable; procures success to the weak, and esteem to all."
– George Washington in Letter of Instructions to the Captains of the Virginia Regiments (29 July 1759).

"Remember that it is the actions, and not the commission, that make the officer, and that there is more expected from him, than the title."
– George Washington in an address to the Officers of the Virginia Regiment, Thursday, January 08, 1756. These words were from an address given when a member of the Virginia Regiment was suspended after he was found

guilty of cheating at a card game while playing with his fellow officers. Washington used this moment to counsel the other soldiers to always maintain self-discipline and behave with honor and integrity.

"My first wish would be that my military family, and the whole Army, should consider themselves as a band of brothers, willing and ready to die for each other."

"If you pick the right people and give them the opportunity to spread their wings and put compensation as a carrier behind it you almost don't have to manage them."

– Jack Welch

## John Wooden

"Many building custodians across the country would tell you that UCLA left the shower and dressing room the cleanest of any team. We picked up all the tape, never was there soap on the shower floor for someone to slip on, made sure all the showers were turned off and all towels were accounted for. The towels were always deposited in a receptacle, if there was one, or stacked nearly near the door. It seems to me that this is everyone's responsibility, not just the manager's. Furthermore, I believe it is a form of discipline that should be a way of life, not to please some building custodian, but as an expression of courtesy and politeness that each of us owes to his fellow man. These little things establish a spirit of togetherness and consideration that help unite the team into a solid unit."

## Wu Qi

"[The general's] reputation, virtues, benevolence and courage must be respected by his subordinates and calm the masses."

"If the soldiers are committed to fighting to death, they will live; if they seek to stay alive, they will die."

## Xenophon

"When on active service, the commander must prove himself conspicuously careful in the matter of forage, quarters, water-supply, outposts, and all other requisites; forecasting the future and keeping ever a wakeful eye in the interest of those under him; and in case of any advantage won, the truest gain which the head of affairs can reap is to share with his men the profits of success."

"After all, you are generals, you are officers and captains. In peace time, you got more pay and respect than they did. Now, in war time, you ought to hold yourselves to be braver than the general mass of men, and to take decisions for the rest, and, if necessary, to be the first to do the hard work."

"If you would stir in each [officer] a personal ambition to appear at the head of his own squadron in all ways splendidly appointed, the best incentive will be your personal example."

"If, further, the men shall see in their commander one who, with the knowledge how to act, has force of will and cunning to make them get the better of the enemy; and if, further, they have got the notion well into their heads that this same leader may be trusted not to lead them recklessly against the foe, without the help of Heaven, or despite the auspices – I say, you have a list of virtues which will make those under his command the more obedient to their ruler."

## Zhang Liang

"The commander-in-chief focuses on winning the minds of the capable, remunerate the meritorious, and having his will adopted by the masses. Thus if he has the same wishes as the masses, there is nothing he cannot accomplish."

"If the general leads the men in person, the soldiers will become the most valiant under Heaven."

"Treating the people as they should be treated shows the greatness of the ruler."

*Dwight D. Eisenhower*

# CHAPTER FOURTEEN

## Favoritism, Confidants, Seeking and Giving Counsel

"The most and best of us depend on others; we have to live either among friends or among enemies."

– Baltasar Gracián

## Aristotle

"It is the mark of an educated mind to be able to entertain a thought without accepting it."

## Marcus Aurelius

"If someone can prove me wrong and show me my mistake in any thought or action, I shall gladly change. I seek the truth, which never harmed anyone: the harm is to persist in one's own self-deception and ignorance."

"Whenever you are about to find fault with someone, ask yourself the following question: What fault of mine most nearly resembles the one I am about to criticize?"

## Arthur James Balfour

"It is unfortunate, considering that enthusiasm moves the world, that so few enthusiasts can be trusted to tell the truth."

## Cato the Elder

"Wise men learn more from fools than fools from the wise."

## Chanakya, The Indian Machiavelli

"Governance is possible only with assistance. A single wheel does not move. Hence ministers [department heads] should be appointed and their counsel listened to."

"In order to develop discipline, one should daily have the company of learned elders, who are firmly rooted in discipline."

"(The ruler) devoid of the power of the counsel, should gather around him a collection of wise men or consult learned elders."

"That which will not be believed, even if it is truth, should not be spoken."

"To as many men a ruler divulges a secret, on so many men he becomes dependent, rendered helpless by the act of his."

"Don't debate with fools."

"Meaningful words, even from a child, should be listened to."

## Winston S. Churchill

"The greatest lesson in life is to know that even fools are right sometimes."

"Criticism may not be agreeable, but it is necessary. It fulfills the same function as pain in the human body; it calls attention to the development of an unhealthy state of things. If it is heeded in time, danger may be averted; if it is suppressed, a fatal distemper may develop."

## W. Edwards Deming

"Without data, you're just another person with an opinion."

"Wise leaders generally have wise counselors because it takes a wise person to distinguish them."

– Diogenes

## Dwight D. Eisenhower

"I know of only one way in which you can be sure you have done your best to make a wise decision. That is to get all of the responsible policymakers with their different viewpoints in front of you, and listen to them debate. I do not believe in bringing them in one at a time, and therefore being more impressed by the most recent one you hear than the earliest ones. You must get courageous men of strong views, and let them debate with each other."

## Epictetus

"Nature has given men one tongue but two ears, that we may hear from others twice as much as we speak."

## Jean de La Fontaine

"Nothing is more dangerous than a friend without discretion; even a prudent enemy is preferable."

## Johann Wolfgang Von Goethe

"To accept advice is but to increase one's own ability."

"The fool and the wise man are equally harmless; it is the half-wise and half-foolish who are to be feared."

## Baltasar Gracián

"When you counsel someone, you should appear to be reminding him of something he had forgotten, not of the light he was unable to see."

## Isocrates

"When there is anything of which you are ashamed to speak openly, but about which you wish to confer with some of your friends, speak as though it were another's affair; thus you will get at their opinion, and will not betray your own case. Whenever you purpose to consult with any one about your affairs, first observe how he has managed his own; for he who has shown poor judgment in conducting his own business will never give wise counsel about the business of others. The greatest incentive you can have to deliberation is to observe the misfortunes which spring from the lack of it; for we pay the closest attention to our health when we recall the pains which spring from disease."
– Isocrates Vol. 1: To Demonicus (34-35).

## Niccolò Machiavelli

"It is an infallible rule that a prince (leader) who is not wise himself cannot be well advised... And it cannot be otherwise, for men will always be false to you unless they are compelled by necessity to be true."

"There is no other way to guard yourself against flattery than by making men understand that telling you the truth will not offend you."

## Lucius Aemilius Paulus

"Commanders should be counseled, chiefly, by persons of known talent, by those who have made an art of war their particular study, and whose knowledge is derived from experience; from those who are present at the scene of action, who see the country, who see the enemy, who see the advantages that occasions offer, and who, like people embarked in the same ship, are sharers of the danger."

"Time is the wisest counselor of all"

– Pericles

## Plato

"They deem him their worst who tells them the truth."

## William Wrigley Jr.

"When two men in a business always agree, one of them is unnecessary."

## Tsunetomo Yamamoto

"To give a person an opinion one must first judge well whether that person is of the disposition to receive it or not."

# CHAPTER FIFTEEN

## On Earning Your Team's Respect

"Respect yourself and others will respect you."

– Confucius

## Alexander the Great

On Alexander the Great: "Now, however, he marched out against Darius, expecting to fight another battle; but when he heard that Darius had been seized by Bessus, he sent his Thessalians home, after distributing among them a largess of two thousand talents over and above their pay. In consequence of the pursuit of Darius, which was long and arduous (for in eleven days he rode thirty-three hundred furlongs (644km), most of his horsemen gave out, and chiefly for lack of water. At this point some Macedonians met him who were carrying water from the river in skins upon their mules. And when they beheld Alexander, it being now midday, in a wretched plight from thirst, they quickly filled a helmet and brought it to him. To his enquiry for whom they were carrying the water, they replied: 'For our own sons; but if thou livest, we can get other sons, even if we lose these.' On hearing this he took the helmet into his hands, but when he looked around and saw the horsemen about him all stretching out their heads and gazing at the water, he handed it back without drinking any, but with praises for the men who had brought it; 'For,' said he, 'if I should drink of it alone, these horsemen of mine will be out of heart.' But when they beheld his self-control and loftiness of spirit, they shouted out to him to lead them forward boldly, and began to goad their horses on, declaring that they would not regard themselves as weary, or thirsty, or as mortals at all, so long as they had such a king."
– Plutarch, Life of Alexander 42.3-6 (Plutarch. Plutarch's

Lives. with an English Translation by. Bernadotte Perrin. Cambridge, MA. Harvard University Press. London. William Heinemann Ltd. 1919. 7.)

"But does any man among you honestly feel that he has suffered more for me than I have suffered for him? Come now, if you are wounded, strip and show your wounds, and I will show mine. There is no part of my body but my back which has not a scar; not a weapon a man may grasp or fling the mark of which I do not carry upon me. I have sword-cuts from close fight; arrows have pierced me, missiles from catapults bruised my flesh; again and again I have been struck by stones or clubs – and all for your sakes: for your glory and gain."

## Warren G. Bennis

"Great groups need to know that the person at the top will fight like a tiger for them."

## Larry Bird

"Leadership is diving for a loose ball, getting the crowd involved, getting other players involved. It's being able to take it as well as dish it out. That's the only way you're going to get respect from the players."

"Leadership is getting players to believe in you. If you tell a teammate you're ready to play as tough as you're able to, you'd better go out there and do it. Players will see right through a phony. And they can tell when you're not giving it all you've got."

## Omar Bradley

"Dependability, integrity, the characteristic of never knowingly doing anything wrong, that you would never cheat anyone, that you would give everybody a fair deal. Character is a sort of an all-inclusive thing. If a man has character, everyone has confidence in him. Soldiers must have confidence in their leader."

## Chanakya, The Indian Machiavelli

"He feeds on nectar, who first feeds his people and then eats the leftovers."

"The one who travels by carriage does not feel the weariness of the journey."

## Confucius

"He does not preach what he practices till he has practiced what he preaches."

*Confucius as imagined by the Ming Dynasty artist Qiu Ying*

## Max De Pree

"Leaders don't inflict pain, they share pain."

## Dwight D. Eisenhower

"Nothing is easy in war. Mistakes are always paid for in casualties and troops are quick to sense any blunder made by their commanders."

"Humility must always be the portion of any man who receives acclaim earned in blood of his followers and sacrifices of his friends."

"You don't lead by hitting people over the head – that's assault, not leadership."

"Don't explain your philosophy. Embody it."

– Epictetus

## Frederick the Great

"If you wish to be loved by your soldiers, husband their blood and do not lead them to slaughter."

## Thomas Fuller

"If you command wisely, you'll be obeyed cheerfully."

## Hannibal Barca

"Now as for me, my men, there is not one of you who has not with his own eyes seen me strike a blow in battle; I have watched and witnessed your valor in the field, and your acts of courage I know by heart, with every detail of when and where they took place: and this, surely, is not a thing of small importance. I was your pupil before I was your commander; I shall advance into the line with soldiers I have a thousand times praised and rewarded; and the enemy we shall meet are raw troops with a raw general, neither knowing anything of the other."

## Dee Hock

"If you don't understand that you work for your mislabeled 'subordinates', then you know nothing of leadership. You know only tyranny."

"Men should be taught and won over by reason, not by blows, insults, and corporal punishments."

– Julian the Apostate

## Michael Jordan

"Earn your leadership every day."

## Jiang Taigong

"If the general is not benevolent, then the army will not be close to or support him. If the general is not courageous, then the army will not be fierce. If the general is not wise, then the army will be in doubts. If the general is not perspicacious, then the army will be confounded. If the general is not quick-witted and acute, then the army will lose the opportunity. If the general is not constantly alert, the army will be weak in defense. If the general is not strong and forceful, then the army will fail in their duty. Thus the general is the Master of Fate. The army is ordered because of him, and they are disordered because of him as well. If one obtains someone who is worthy to serve as general, the army will be strong and the state will prosper. If one does not obtain a worthy as general, the army will be weak and state will perish."

## Ingvar Kamprad

"If there is such a thing as good leadership, it is to give a good example. I have to do so for all the Ikea employees."

## Herb Kelleher

"If the employees come first, then they're happy. A motivated employee treats the customer well. The customer is happy so they keep coming back, which pleases the shareholders. It's not one of the enduring green mysteries of all time, it is just the way it works."

"Treat your employees like customers."

## Tom Landry

"Leadership is a matter of having people look at you and gain confidence, seeing how you react. If you're in control, they're in control."

**Abraham Lincoln**

"If you once forfeit the confidence of your fellow citizens, you can never regain their respect and esteem. It is true that you may fool all of the people some of the time; you can even fool some of the people all of the time; but you can't fool all of the people all of the time.

– From a speech given by Abraham Lincoln at Clinton, Illinois, September 8, 1854.

**Jack Ma**

"I don't want to be liked. I want to be respected."

**Niccolò Machiavelli**

"You will always need the favor of the inhabitants... It is necessary for a prince to possess the friendship of the people."

**Audie Murphy**

"Lead from the front."

> "The greatest gift you can give another is the purity of your attention."
>
> – Pericles

## Erwin Rommel

"The commander must try, above all, to establish personal and comradely contact with his men, but without giving away an inch of his authority."

"Courage which goes against military expediency is stupidity, or, if it is insisted upon by a commander, irresponsibility."

"Be an example to your men, in your duty and in private life. Never spare yourself, and let the troops see that you don't in your endurance of fatigue and privation. Always be tactful and well-mannered and teach your subordinates to do the same. Avoid excessive sharpness or harshness of voice, which usually indicates the man who has shortcomings of his own to hide."

*Firld Marshal Erwin Rommel*

## Junior Seau

"Leadership can't be fabricated. If it is fabricated and rehearsed, you can't fool the guys in the locker room. So when you talk about leadership, it comes with performance. Leadership comes with consistency."

"People want guidance, not rhetoric. They need to know what the plan of action is, and how it will be implemented. They want to be given responsibility to help solve the problem and authority to act on it."

– Howard Schultz

## Sun Bin

"Commanders must have integrity; without integrity, they have no power. If they have no power, they cannot bring out the best in their armies. Therefore, integrity is the hand of warriorship."

## Sun Tzu

"The general must be first in the toils and fatigues of the army. In the heat of summer he does not spread his parasol, nor in the cold of winter don thick clothing... He waits until the army's wells have been dug and only then drinks; until the army's food is cooked before he eats; until the army's fortifications have been completed, to shelter himself."

"Pay heed to nourishing the troops; do not unnecessarily fatigue them. Unite them in spirit; conserve their strength. Make unfathomable plans for the movement of the army. Thus, such troops need no encouragement to be vigilant. Without extorting their support the general obtains it; without inviting their affection he gains it; without demanding their trust he wins it."

## Tacitus

"In the election of kings they have regard to birth; in that of generals, to valor. Their kings have not an absolute or unlimited power; and their generals command less through the force of authority, than of example. If they are daring, adventurous, and conspicuous in action, they procure obedience from the admiration they inspire."

– Tacitus, on the Germanic warriors.

## Jack Welch

"When you were made a leader you weren't given a crown, you were given the responsibility to bring out the best in others."

## John Wooden

"I remain convinced to this day that compassion like that
– sincerely caring for your players and maintaining an
active interest in their lives, concerns, and motivations –
is one of the most important qualities a coach can have."

## Xenophon

"If, further, the men shall see in their commander one
who, with the knowledge how to act, has force of will
and cunning to make them get the better of the enemy;
and if, further, they have got the notion well into their
heads that this same leader may be trusted not to lead
them recklessly against the foe, without the help of
Heaven, or despite the auspices – I say, you have a list of
virtues which will make those under his command the
more obedient to their ruler."

"You must endeavor to make your practice correspond
with what you preach."

"Where there is no-one in control, nothing useful or
distinguished can ever get done."

## Zhang Liang

"If you dismiss one good man, then all good people will lose heart. Reward an evil person and all evil persons will be drawn to you."

"Now those who command the army must share joy and sorrow with the officers and men, and confront safety and danger with them. Only then can they confront the enemy, gained full victory and the enemy completely destroyed."

# CHAPTER SIXTEEN

## On Managing Your Image and Creating a Mystique

"You are one of the rare people who can separate your observation from your preconception. You see what is, where most people see what they expect."

– John Steinbeck, East of Eden

## Nolan Bushnell

"Pretend to be completely in control and people will assume that you are."

## Julius Caesar

"As a rule, what is out of sight disturbs men's minds more seriously than what they see."

"In the end, it is impossible not to become what others believe you are." (Attributed to Julius Caesar.)

## Cicero

"Who does not know that what the enemy, what the allies think of our general, is greatly of relevance to waging war, since we know that human beings are moved by belief and hearsay no less than by any specific reason in matters of such importance that they either despise or fear, either hate or love? Which name, then, has ever been more famous in the whole wide world? Whose deeds comparable? About which man have you passed such weighty and such glorious judgments, which is the greatest source of authority?"

– Cicero On the Command of Pompey The Great.

"If you have no confidence in yourself, you are twice defeated in the race of life. With confidence, you have won even before you have started."

*Marcus Tullius Cicero*
*First-century AD bust in the Capitoline Museums, Rome*

**Epictetus**

"Know, first, who you are, and then adorn yourself accordingly."

"Don't explain your philosophy. Embody it."

"You can't build a reputation on what you're going to do."

– Henry Ford

**Baltasar Gracián**

"Folly consists not in committing folly, but in being incapable of concealing it. All men make mistakes, but the wise conceal the blunders they have made, while fools make them public. Reputation depends more on what is hidden than on what is seen. If you can't be good, be careful."

"Never have a companion that casts you in the shade."

# Hadrian

"Hadrian's memory was vast and his ability was unlimited; for instance, he personally dictated his speeches and gave opinions on all questions. He was also very witty, and of his jests many still survive. The following one has even become famous: When he had refused a request to a certain grey-haired man, and the man repeated the request but this time with dyed hair, Hadrian replied: "I have already refused this to your father." Even without the aid of a nomenclator he could call by name a great many people, whose names he had heard but once and then all in a crowd; indeed, he could correct the nomenclators when they made mistakes, as they not infrequently did, and he even knew the names of the veterans whom he had discharged at various times. He could repeat from memory, after a rapid reading, books which to most men were not known at all. He wrote, dictated, listened, and, incredible as it seems, conversed with his friends, all at one and the same time. He had as complete a knowledge of the state-budget in all its details as any careful householder has of his own household."

– Description of the Roman emperor Hadrian. Historia Augusta, Life of Hadrian 20.1, 7-12.

# Thomas Jefferson

"The most valuable of all talents is that of never using two words when one will do."

"On matters of style, swim with the current, on matters of principle, stand like a rock."

"Confidence is contagious. So is lack of confidence."

– Vince Lombardi Jr.

## Abraham Lincoln

"When I get ready to talk to people, I spend two thirds of the time thinking what they want to hear and one third thinking about what I want to say."

"Character is like a tree and reputation its shadow. The shadow is what we think it is and the tree is the real thing."

## Niccolò Machiavelli

"Everyone sees what you appear to be, few experience what you really are."

"Therefore it is unnecessary for a prince to have all the good qualities I have enumerated, but it is very necessary to appear to have them. And I shall dare to say this also, that to have them and always to observe them is injurious, and that to appear to have them is useful; to appear merciful, faithful, humane, religious, upright, and to be so, but with a mind so framed that should you require not to be so, you may be able and know how to change to the opposite."

"And here comes in the question whether it is better to be loved rather than feared, or feared rather than loved. It might perhaps be answered that we should wish to be both; but since love and fear can hardly exist together, if we must choose between them, it is far safer to be feared than loved... It is much safer to be feared than loved because... love is preserved by the link of obligation which, owing to the baseness of men, is broken at every opportunity for their advantage; but fear preserves you by a dread of punishment which never fails."

"The vulgar crowd always is taken by appearances, and the world consists chiefly of the vulgar."

## George S. Patton

"It may well be that the greatest soldiers have possessed superior intellects, may have been thinkers; but this was not their dominant characteristic. With the possible exception of Moltke, all great generals with whom we are familiar owed their success to indomitable wills and tremendous energy in execution and they achieved their initial hold upon the hearts of their troops by acts of demonstrated valor."

## François de La Rochefoucauld

"We do not despise all those with vices, but we do despise all those without a single virtue."

## Harry S. Truman

"I never did give them hell. I just told the truth, and they thought it was hell."

## George Washington

"Associate yourself with men of good quality if you esteem your own reputation. It is better be alone than in bad company."

# CHAPTER SEVENTEEN

## Motivating Your Team

"A team aligned behind a vision will move mountains."

– Kevin Rose

## Alexander the Great

"But does any man among you honestly feel that he has suffered more for me than I have suffered for him? Come now – if you are wounded, strip and show your wounds, and I will show mine. There is no part of my body but my back which has not a scar; not a weapon a man may grasp or fling the mark of which I do not carry upon me. I have sword-cuts from close fight; arrows have pierced me, missiles from catapults bruised my flesh; again and again I have been struck by stones or clubs – and all for your sakes: for your glory and gain."

"I am not afraid of an army of lions led by a sheep; I am afraid of an army of sheep led by a lion."

## Mary Kay Ash

"Never giving criticism without praise is a strict rule for me. No matter what you are criticizing, you must find something good to say – both before and after... Criticize the act, not the person"

"We treat our people like royalty. If you honor and serve the people who work for you, they will honor and serve you."

"Everyone has an invisible sign hanging from their neck saying, 'Make me feel important.' Never forget this message when working with people."

"A mediocre idea that generates enthusiasm will go further than a great idea that inspires no one."

## John C. "Doc" Bahnsen

"True caring about others is the critical element that translates the personality of a leader into the catalyst that results in charismatic leadership. Caring consists of a genuine understanding for the needs and aspirations of others and a demonstrated willingness to act on their behalf. Mere words are not enough. Caring starts by looking others in the eye and you talk to them and listening to them when they talk to you. Charismatic leaders are also outstanding mentors and developers of their subordinates. This ability springs from a corresponding desire to have successful, highly motivated people working for you."

## Frederick "Boots" Blesse

"No guts, no glory."

## Jean de la Bruyère

"The shortest and best way to make your fortune is to let people see clearly that it is in their interests to promote yours."

**Bear Bryant**

"I know my players better than they know themselves. How else could I get the best out of them?"

> "I like to praise and reward in a loud voice and to scold in a whisper."
>
> – Catherine the Great

**Bennett Cerf**

"A pat on the back, though only a few vertebrae removed from a kick in the pants, is miles ahead in results."

**Chanakya, The Indian Machiavelli**

"He who punishes severely is hated by the people. He who punishes mildly is despised. One who metes out deserving punishment is respected."

"When the tasks are great, abundant rewards should be made the incentive."

## Chinese Proverb

"Not the cry, but the flight of the wild duck, leads the flock to fly and follow."

– Chinese Proverb

## Winston Churchill

"It is not enough that we do our best; sometimes we must do what is required."

"Before you can inspire with emotion, you must be swamped with it yourself. Before you can move their tears, your own must flow. To convince them, you must yourself believe."

## Cuthbert Collingwood

"Now, gentlemen, let us do something today which the world may talk of hereafter."

– Vice Admiral Collingwood before the Battle of Trafalgar, October 21, 1805.

*Vice Admiral Cuthbert Collingwood, 1st Baron Collingwood*

## Charles De Gaulle

"It is, indeed, an observable fact that all leaders of men, whether as political figures, prophets, or soldiers, all those who can get the best out of others, have always identified themselves with high ideals."

## Peter Drucker

"Leadership is lifting a person's vision to high sights, the raising of a person's performance to a higher standard, the building of a personality beyond its normal limitations."

## Demosthenes

"All speech is vain and empty unless it be accompanied by action."

## Ralph Waldo Emerson

"Our chief want is someone who will inspire us to be what we know we could be."

## Queen Elizabeth I

"And therefore I am come amongst you at this time, not as for my recreation or sport, but being resolved, in the midst and heat of the battle, to live or die amongst you all; to lay down, for my God, and for my kingdom, and for my people, my honour and my blood, even the dust. I know I have but the body of a weak and feeble woman; but I have the heart of a king, and of a king of England, too."

– Queen Elizabeth I in a speech to the troops at Tilbury in Essex as preparation were being made for repelling the imminent invasion by the Spanish Armada in 1588.

## Frederick the Great

"It has been said by a certain general, that the first object in the establishment of an army ought to be making provision for the belly, that being the basis and foundation of all operations."

## Harold S. Geneen

"The best way to inspire people to superior performance is to convince them by everything you do and by your everyday attitude that you are wholeheartedly supporting them."

## Genghis Khan

"One arrow alone can be easily broken but many arrows are indestructible."

– Genghis Khan's speech to unite the Mongol tribes.

"Heaven has abandoned China owing to its haughtiness and extravagant luxury. But I, living in the northern wilderness, have not inordinate passions. I hate luxury and exercise moderation. I have only one coat and one food. I eat the same food and am dressed in the same tatters as my humble herdsmen. I consider the people my children, and take an interest in talented men as if they were my brothers. We always agree in our principles, and we are always united by mutual affection. At military exercises I am always in front, and in time of battle am never behind. In the space of seven years I have succeeded in accomplishing a great work, and uniting the whole world in one empire."
– Genghis Khan speaking to his army.

"Treat people as if they were what they ought to be, and you help them become what they are capable of being."

– Johann Wolfgang von Goethe

## Thomas Fuller

"If you command wisely, you'll be obeyed cheerfully."

## Louis V. Gerstner, Jr.

"I think that my leadership style is to get people to fear staying in place, to fear not changing."

## Hannibal

"We have nothing left in the world but what we can win with our swords. Timidity and cowardice are for men who can see safety at their backs; who can retreat without molestation along some easy road and find refuge in the familiar fields of their native land; but they are not for you: you must be brave; for you there is no middle way between victory or death – put all hope of it from you, and either conquer, or, should fortune hesitate to favor you, meet death in battle rather than in flight."

## Patrick Henry

"The battle, sir, is not to the strong alone; it is to the vigilant, the active, the brave."

## Special Forces/Delta Operator MSG Paul R. Howe

"Your job as a team leader is to "live the example" for all to see and aspire to be."

## Lee Iacocca

"I've always felt that a manager has achieved a great deal when he's able to motivate one other person. When it comes to making the place run, motivation is everything. You might be able to do the work of two people, but you can't be two people. Instead, you have to inspire the next guy down the line and get him to inspire his people."

## Reggie Jackson

"I'll tell you what makes a great manager: A great manager has a knack for making ballplayers think they are better than they think they are. He forces you to have a good opinion of yourself. He lets you know he believes in you. He makes you get more out of yourself. And once you learn how good you really are, you never settle for playing anything less than your very best."

## Stonewall Jackson

"I yield to no man in sympathy for the gallant men under my command, but I am obliged to sweat them tonight,

235

so that I may save their blood tomorrow."

**Lyndon B. Johnson**

"What convinces is conviction. Believe in the argument you're advancing. If you don't, you're as good as dead. The other person will sense that something isn't there, and no chain of reasoning, no matter how logical or elegant or brilliant, will win your case for you."

> "One person can make a difference and every person should try."
>
> – John F Kennedy

**Tommy Lasorda**

"Players are like snowflakes or fingerprints. There are no two alike. You have to handle them all different. Some guys, in order to get their attention, you have to holler at them and fine them. There are other guys you can't. Some guys you holler at them, they crawl into a shell. Some guys you holler at them, they lose their confidence. You gotta always try to do everything you can to help them maintain that confidence level."

## Vince Lombardi Jr.

"Individual commitment to a group effort; that is what makes a team work, a company work, a society work, a civilization work."

"Gentlemen, we will chase perfection, and we will chase it relentlessly, knowing all the while we can never attain it. But along the way, we shall catch excellence."

"Once you learn to quit, it becomes a habit."

## Abraham Lincoln

"In this and like communities, public sentiment is everything. With public sentiment, nothing can fail; without it nothing can succeed. Consequently he who molds public sentiment, goes deeper than he who enacts statutes or pronounces decisions. He makes statutes and decisions possible or impossible to be executed."

"You cannot build character and courage by taking away people's initiative and independence."

## Nelson Mandela

"It is better to lead from behind and to put others in front, especially when you celebrate victory when nice things occur. You take the front line when there is danger. Then people will appreciate your leadership."

## Horace Mann

"A teacher who is attempting to teach without inspiring the pupil with a desire to learn is hammering on cold iron."

## Niccolò Machiavelli

"Men are driven by two principal impulses, either by love or by fear."

"He who becomes a Prince through the favor of the people should always keep on good terms with them; which it is easy for him to do, since all they ask is not to be oppressed."

## Mencius

"Let men decide firmly what they will not do, and they will be free to do vigorously what they ought to do."

## Dr. Charles McMoran Wilson

"A few men had the stuff of leadership in them, they were like rafts to which all the rest of humanity clung for support and hope."

## Audi Murphy

"Lead from the front."

## Miyamoto Musashi

"The only reason a warrior is alive is to fight, and the only reason a warrior fights is to win"

## Napoleon I

"A leader is a dealer of hope."

"Men are more easily governed through their vices than through their virtues."

"Men are Moved by two levers only: fear and self-interest."

"Impossible is a word to be found only in the dictionary of fools."

"One obtains everything from men by appealing to their sense of honor."

## William Oncken Jr.

"Your character, as a source of managerial influence, is the degree to which others respect your personal commitment not to allow them to wind up with the short end of the stick if they take you at your word. If they do not see such a personal commitment as characteristic of you, then to that extent, your influence will be weakened."

## George Orwell

"High sentiments always win in the end. The leaders who offer blood, toil, tears and sweat always get more out of their followers than those who offer safety and a good time. When it comes to the pinch, human beings are heroic."

## Pericles

"Thus choosing to die resisting, rather than to live submitting, they fled only from dishonor, but met danger face to face, and after one brief moment, while at the summit of their fortune, left behind them not their fear, but their glory."

– Pericles's funeral oration for Athenian soldiers.

## Eva Perón

"One cannot accomplish anything without fanaticism."

"Soldier's bellies are not satisfied with empty promises and hopes."

– Peter the Great

## Plutarch

"The Spartans do not ask how many are the enemy but where are they."

## Pierre-Joseph Proudhon

"When deeds speak, words are nothing."

## Howard Schultz

"One of the fundamental aspects of leadership, I realized more and more, is the ability to instill confidence in others when you yourself are feeling insecure."

## Ernest Henry Shackleton

"Fortitudine Vincimus – By Endurance We Conquer."

– Favorite quote of Sir Ernest Henry Shackleton.

## Albert Schweitzer

"Example is not the main thing in influencing others. It is the only thing."

## Sam Walton

"Nothing else can quite substitute for a few well-chosen, well-timed, sincere words of praise. They're absolutely free and worth a fortune."

"Outstanding leaders go out of their way to boost the self-esteem of their personnel. If people believe in themselves, it's amazing what they can accomplish."

### Antoine de Saint-Exupery

"If you want to build a ship, don't drum up people to collect wood and don't assign them tasks and work, but rather teach them to long for the endless immensity of the sea."

### George Washington

"A people unused to restraint must be led, they will not be drove."
– George Washington in a letter to Major General Stirling, Sunday, January 19, 1777, on repudiating the harsh disciplinary methods used on British and Hessian troops. He felt they would be detrimental to his Continental Army.

### Jack Welch

"Take every opportunity to inject self-confidence into those who have earned it. Use ample praise, the more specific the better."

### Xenophon

"The leader must himself believe that willing obedience always beats forced obedience, and that he can get this only by really knowing what should be done. Thus he can secure obedience from his men because he can convince them that he knows best, precisely as a good doctor makes his patients obey him.

"An officer must be competent to so assert himself in speech or action so that those under him will no longer hesitate. They will recognize of themselves that it is a good thing and a right to obey, to follow their leader, to rush to close quarters with the foe. A desire will consume them to achieve some deed of glory and renown. A capacity will be given them patiently to abide by the resolution of their souls."

## Zhang Liang

"One does not employ righteous officers using solely material wealth. This is because the righteous will not die for the malevolent."

"If the general is not brave, his officers and men will be terrified. If the general moves the army recklessly, the army will not be imposing. If his anger implicates the innocent, the whole army will be in fear."

# CHAPTER EIGHTEEN

## On Delegation and Giving Orders

"The best executive is the one who has sense enough to pick good men to do what he wants done, and self-restraint to keep from meddling while they do it."

– Theodore Roosevelt

## Alexander the Great

"To the strongest."

– Alexander the Great, answering the question who he would leave his empire after his death.

## John Adams

"Power must never be trusted without a check."

## Julius Caesar

"The situation was saved by two things – first, the knowledge and experience of the soldiers, whose training in earlier battles enabled them to decide for themselves what needed doing, without waiting to be told; secondly, the order which Caesar had issued to all his generals, not to leave the work but to stay each with his own legion... As the enemy was so close and advancing so swiftly, the generals did not wait for further orders but on their own responsibility took the measures they thought proper."

– Julius Caesar, The Conquest of Gaul.

*John Adams*

## Queen Elizabeth I

"A strength to harm is perilous in the hand of an ambitious head."

## Henry Ford

Asking "Who ought to be boss?" is like asking "Who ought to be the tenor in the quartet?" Obviously, the man who can sing tenor."

"Freedom is not worth having if it does not include the freedom to make mistakes."

– Mahatma Gandhi

## Genghis Khan

"Those who were adept and brave fellows I have made military commanders. Those who were quick and nimble I have made herders of horses. Those who were not adept I have given a small whip and sent to be shepherds."

## Dee Hock

"It is essential to employ, trust, and reward those whose perspective, ability, and judgment are radically different from yours. It is also rare, for it requires uncommon humility, tolerance, and wisdom."

## Stonewall Jackson

"Don't say it's impossible! Turn your command over to the next officer. If he can't do it, I'll find someone who can, even if I have to take him from the ranks!"

## Jiang Taigong

"You should make your commands clear and be careful about your orders."

## Helmuth Karl Bernhard Moltke

"Remember gentlemen, an order than can be misunderstood will be misunderstood."

## George S. Patton Jr.

"Never tell people how to do things. Tell them what to do and they will surprise you with their ingenuity."

## Don Peterson

Ford Motor Company pushes decision making "...as far down in the organization as we think we possibly can, on the very sound principle that the farther down you get, the closer you're getting to where there's true knowledge about the issues."

## Plutarch

"To find fault is easy; to do better may be difficult."

## Hyman G. Rickover

"Human experience shows that people, not organizations or management systems, get things done. For this reason, subordinates must be given authority and responsibility early in their careers. In this way they develop quickly and can help the manager do his work. The manager, of course, remains ultimately responsible and must accept the blame if subordinates make mistakes."

## Teddy Roosevelt

"Each man was summoned before Roosevelt and told in no uncertain terms that there would be only one boss. "Colonel Goethals here is to be chairman," said the president. "He is to have complete authority. If at any time you do not agree with his policies, do not bother to tell me about it – your disagreement with him will constitute your resignation."

– Teddy Roosevelt speaking to the Panama Canal team when he put George Washington Goethals in charge of the Panama Canal project which until this point had been in disarray. From the book 'The Path Between the Seas: The Creation of the Panama Canal, 1870-1914' by David McCullough.

## Sun Tzu

"A sovereign of high character and intelligence must be able to know the right man, should place the responsibility on him, and expect results."

## George Washington

"It is absolutely necessary... for me to have persons that can think for me, as well as execute orders."

## Lillian Vernon

"Understand the art of management. Some entrepreneurs are so creative and committed to their business, they fail to delegate responsibilities to others, which can lead to failure. Hire talented employees who can carry out the nuts and bolts of your business. Let them share responsibility in the decision-making process. Keep an open mind, hear their ideas and suggestions first before you turn down their proposals. You can oversee all aspects of your company while they are involved as well."

# CHAPTER NINETEEN

## On Betrayal

"I lay it down as a fact that if all men knew what others say of them, there would not be four friends in the world."

– Blaise Pascal

## Baldassare Castiglione

"Thus for my own part I have more than once been deceived by the person I loved most and of whose love, above everyone else's, I have been most confident; and because of this I have sometimes thought to myself that it may be as well to never trust anyone in this world nor to give oneself as a hostage to a friend, however dear and cherished he may be, to the extent of telling him all one's thoughts without reserve as if he were one's very self. For there are so many concealed places and recesses in our minds that it is humanly impossible to discover and judge the pretenses hidden there. So that I believe that it might be right to love and serve one person above all others, according to merit and worth, but never to trust so much in this tempting trap of friendship as to have to cause to repent of it later on."

## Chanakya, The Indian Machiavelli

"The evil one harms, even if treated well."

"Even after wealth has been acquired, an enemy should not be trusted."

"It is better not to have a ruler than have a bad ruler. It is better to not have a friend, than have a bad friend. It is better to not have a disciple rather than have a bad disciple. It is better not to have a wife rather than have a bad wife."

"To as many men a ruler divulges a secret, on so many men he becomes dependent, rendered helpless by the act of his."

## Viktor E. Frankl

"No man should judge unless he asks himself in absolute honesty whether in a similar situation he might not have done the same."

## Benjamin Franklin

"Three may keep a secret, if two of them are dead."

## Basil Liddell Hart

"Those who are naturally loyal say little about it, and are ready to assume it in others. In contrast, the type of soldier who is always dwelling on the importance of 'loyalty' usually means loyalty to his own interests."

## Martin Luther King Jr.

"There comes a time when silence is betrayal."

**Eleanor Roosevelt**

"If someone betrays you once, it's their fault; if they betray you twice, it's your fault."

**Tacitus**

"Men are more ready to repay an injury than a benefit, because gratitude is a burden and revenge a pleasure."

**George Washington**

"I had no conception... that every act of my administration would be tortured... in such exaggerated form and indecent terms as could scarcely be applied to a Nero, a notorious defaulter or even a common pickpocket."

– George Washington in his last letter to Thomas Jefferson.

# CHAPTER TWENTY

## On Mentoring
## and Teaching Leadership

"The mind is not a vessel to be filled, but a fire to be kindled."

– Plutarch

## Alexander the Great

"I am indebted to my father for living, but to my teacher for living well."
(One of Alexander's tutors was Aristotle.)

"When we give someone our time, we actually give a portion of our life that we will never take back."

"I had rather excel others in the knowledge of what is excellent, than in the extent of my power and dominion."

## Marcus Aurelius

"All men are made one for another: either then teach them better or bear with them."

## Bill Bradley

"Leadership is unlocking people's potential to become better."

## Benjamin Franklin

"Tell me and I forget, teach me and I may remember, involve me and I learn."

> "The growth and development of people is the highest calling of leadership."
>
> – Harvey S. Firestone

## Frederick Douglass

"It is easier to build strong children than to repair broken men."

## Thomas Huxley

"The great end of life is not knowledge, but action. What men need is as much knowledge as they can organize for action; give them more and it may become injurious. Some men are heavy and stupid from indigested learning."

## John A. Lejeune

"The relationship between officers and men should in no sense be that of superior and inferior, nor that of master and servant, but rather that of teacher and scholar. In fact, it should partake of the nature of the relationship between father and son, to the extent that officers, especially commanding officers, are responsible for the physical, mental, and moral welfare, as well as the discipline and military training of the young men under their command."

## Abraham Lincoln

"I'm a success today because I had a friend who believed in me and I didn't have the heart to let him down."

"You have to do your own growing no matter how tall your grandfather was."

"I am not concerned that you have fallen; I am concerned that you arise."

## John P. Kotter

"Because management deals mostly with the status quo and leadership deals mostly with change, in the next century we are going to have to try to become much more skilled at creating leaders."

## Jack Ma

"Help young people. Help small guys. Because small

guys will be big. Young people will have the seeds you bury in their minds, and when they grow up, they will change the world."

## Nelson Mandela

"If you talk to a man in a language he understands, that goes to his head. If you talk to him in his language, that goes to his heart."

## George Smith Patton Jr.

"Untutored courage is useless in the face of educated bullets."

## Vegetius

"For as the well trained soldier is eager for action, so does the untaught fear it."

## William Arthur Ward

"The mediocre teacher tells. The good teacher explains. The superior teacher demonstrates. The great teacher inspires."

## George Washington

"A primary object should be the education of our youth in the science of government. In a republic, what species of knowledge can be equally important? And what duty more pressing than communicating it to those who are to be the future guardians of the liberties of the country?"

## Jack Welch

"Before you are a leader, success is all about growing yourself. When you become a leader, success is all about growing others."

## John Wooden

"A coach is someone who can give correction without causing resentment."

# CHAPTER TWENTY-ONE

## On Firing and Being Fired
## and Coping with Defeat

"Victory has a hundred fathers
and defeat is an orphan."

– John F. Kennedy

## Chanakya, The Indian Machiavelli

"The occasions when one should leave one's post are (a) when one's work gets destroyed without fruition, (b) one's power gets reduced, (c) when one's learning is treated like a tradable commodity, (d) one's hopes are frustrated, (e) when one loses the confidence of the master, (g) when one comes into conflict with powerful people."

"The intelligent have no fear about their livelihood."

## Hannibal

"The greater a man's success the less it must be trusted to endure."

– Hannibal Barca to Scipio Africanus (Publius Cornelius Scipio) during a meeting of the two brilliant commanders a day before they were to meet in battle. (The War with Hannibal: The History of Rome from its Foundation, Books 21-30 By Titus Livy).

## Steve Jobs

"I didn't see it then, but it turned out that getting fired from Apple was the best thing that could have ever happened to me. The heaviness of being successful was replaced by the lightness of being a beginner again, less sure about everything. It freed me to enter one of the most creative periods of my life."

– Commencement address delivered by Steve Jobs, CEO of Apple Computer and of Pixar Animation Studios, on June 12, 2005 at Stanford University.

> "I have always found that mercy bears richer fruits than strict justice."
>
> – Abraham Lincoln

## Niccolò Machiavelli

"If an injury has to be done to a man it should be so severe that his vengeance need not be feared."

## Elon Musk

"It's important to tell people why someone was fired. Otherwise, they may think that it was a random decision and not based on merit."

## Jack Welch

"The final relationship that cannot be ignored is with disrupters: They are individuals who cause trouble for sport; inciting opposition to management for a variety of reasons, most of them petty. Usually these people have good performance. That's their cove, and so they are endured or appeased. A company that manages people well takes disrupters head-on. First they give them very tough evaluations, naming their bad behavior and demanding it change. Usually it won't. Disrupters are a personality type. If that's the case, get them out of the way of people trying to do their jobs. They're poison."

## Zhang Liang

"If you dismiss one good man, then all good people will lose heart. Reward an evil person and all evil persons will be drawn to you."

# CHAPTER TWENTY-TWO

## On Bad Leadership

"You cannot get well in a sick organization."

– Unknown

## Chanakya, The Indian Machiavelli

"The ruler who without reason gets angry with his servant attracts the poison (retaliation), as if bitten by a black cobra."

"By excessively cruel punishment, (the ruler) becomes hated by all."

"Evil speech, though unintended, remains long in memory."

## Confucius

"To lead uninstructed people to war is to throw them away."

"In vain I have looked for a single man capable of seeing his own faults and bringing the charge home against himself."

## On General George Custer

"Warfare on the plains demanded flexibility, responsiveness and initiative by those in the front lines of battle, traits Custer almost systematically weeded out of his troops."
– Sitting Bull biographer Emmet Murphy from the book, "The Genius of Sitting Bull."

## Mary Parker Follett

"One of the primary ways leaders contribute to an unethical and potentially corrupt organization is by failing to speak up against acts they believe are wrong. A leader who holds his tongue in order to fit in is essentially giving his or her support for unethical behavior. If a leader knows someone is being treated unfairly by a colleague and does nothing, the leader is setting a precedent to others to behave unfairly as well. Peers and subordinates with lax ethical standards often feel free to act as they choose. It is often hard to stand up for what is right, but this is a primary way in which leaders create an environment of integrity."

## Special Forces/Delta Operator MSG Paul R. Howe

"Poor leadership in the business world will cost you time and money. In the military and law enforcement world, it will cost the lives of mothers, fathers, sons and daughters."

"Much of the problem with the commander's combat mindset mental programming is that they are rarely faced with the immediate threats and violence of action that the troops face on a daily basis."

## Onasander

"The general should be a man of good reputation, because the majority of men, when placed under the command of unknown generals, feel uneasy. For no-one voluntarily submits to a leader or an officer who is an inferior man to himself. It is absolutely essential, then, that a general be such a man, of such excellent traits of character as I have mentioned, and besides this, that he have a good reputation."

– Onasander, 'The General'

## John "Black Jack" Pershing

"A competent leader can get efficient service from poor troops, while an incapable leader can demoralize the best of troops."

## Norman Schwarzkopf

"You learn far more from negative leadership than from positive leadership. Because you learn how not to do it. And, therefore, you learn how to do it."

## John "Jocko" Willink

"The most fundamental and important truths at the heart of Extreme Ownership (his leadership philosophy): there are no bad teams, only bad leaders."

## Sun Tzu

"There are five dangerous faults which may affect a general: (1) Recklessness, which leads to destruction; (2) Cowardice, which leads to capture; (3) A hasty temper, which can be provoked by insults; (4) A delicacy of honor which is sensitive to shame; (5) Over-solicitude for his men, which exposes him to worry and trouble. These are the five besetting sins of a general, ruinous to the conduct of war. When an army is overthrown and its leader slain, the cause will surely be found among these five dangerous faults. Let them be a subject of meditation."

"It is better to offer no excuse than a bad one."

– George Washington

## Zhang Liang

"If the general refuses to ask and listen to advice, then those that are capable will leave. If he refuses to take into consideration any plans set out by strategists, the strategists will leave. If good and evil are treated alike, the meritorious will grow weary. If the general is stubborn, his subordinates will shirk all responsibility. If he brags, his assistants will not attempt any accomplishments. If he believes slander, he will lose the hearts of the people. If he is greedy, treachery will be unchecked. If he is licentious, his officers and men will follow suit. If the general has one of the faults mentioned here, the masses will not submit. If he has two of them, the army will lack discipline. If he has three of them, his subordinates will not fight. If he has four of them, the entire state is in danger."

# PART THREE

# MASTERING

# A LEADERSHIP MINDSET

*Official portrait of John F. Kennedy*

# CHAPTER TWENTY-THREE

## On The Leadership Mindset

"To be a slave to pleasure is the life of a harlot, not a man."

– Anaxandridas II, Spartan King and father of Leonidas I

## Marcus Aurelius

"Begin each day by telling yourself: Today I shall be meeting with interference, ingratitude, insolence, disloyalty, ill-will, and selfishness – all of them due to the offenders' ignorance of what is good or evil."

"A person's worth is measured by the worth of what he values."

"What then is worth being valued? To be received with clapping of hands? No. Neither must we value the clapping of tongues; for the praise which comes from the many is a clapping of tongues. Suppose then that thou hast given up this worthless thing called fame, what remains that is worth valuing? This, in my opinion: to move thyself and to restrain thyself in conformity to thy proper constitution, to which end both all employments and arts lead."

## Boethius

"In other living creatures the ignorance of themselves is nature, but in men it is a vice."

## Tsukahara Bokuden

"Mental bearing (calmness), not skill, is the sign of a matured Samurai. A Samurai therefore should neither be pompous nor arrogant."

## Cato the Elder

"The worst ruler is one who cannot rule himself."

## Cicero

"Six mistakes mankind keeps making century after century: Believing that personal gain is made by crushing others; Worrying about things that cannot be changed or corrected; Insisting that a thing is impossible because we cannot accomplish it; Refusing to set aside trivial preferences; Neglecting development and refinement of the mind; Attempting to compel others to believe and live as we do."

## Dwight D. Eisenhower

"Humility must always be the portion of any man who receives acclaim earned in the blood of his followers and the sacrifices of his friends."

## Epictetus

"Any person capable of angering you becomes your master; he can anger you only when you permit yourself to be disturbed by him."

> "Leadership is practiced not so much in words as in attitude and in actions."
>
> – Harold S. Geneen

## Baltasar Gracián

"Be first the master of yourself"

## Dee Hock

"Through the years, I have greatly feared and sought to keep at bay the four beasts that inevitably devour their keeper – Ego, Envy, Avarice, and Ambition. In 1984, I severed all connections with business for a life of isolation and anonymity, convinced I was making a great bargain by trading money for time, position for liberty, and ego for contentment – that the beasts were securely caged."

## Special Forces/Delta Operator MSG Paul R. Howe

On developing a combat mindset: "I am going to fucking destroy you," is the thought I firmly and quietly placed in my mind along with a game face of focused determination when I was preparing for a combat mission or doing rehearsals with role players. I treated both rehearsals and combat the same for simplicity's sake."

## Tony Hsieh

"Personally I cringe at the word 'leader.' It's more about getting people do what they're passionate about and putting them in the right context or setting. They're the ones doing the hard work."

## Thomas Jefferson

"...above all things lose no occasion of exercising your dispositions to be grateful, to be generous, to be charitable, to be humane, to be true, just, firm, orderly, courageous, etc. Consider every act of this kind as an exercise which will strengthen your moral faculties, & increase your worth."

– Letter from Thomas Jefferson to Peter Carr, August 10th 1787.

A Decalogue of Canons for Observation in Practical Life:

1. Never put off to tomorrow what you can do to-day.
2. Never trouble another with what you can do yourself.
3. Never spend your money before you have it.
4. Never buy a thing you do not want, because it is cheap, it will be dear to you.
5. Take care of your cents: dollars will take care of themselves.
6. Pride costs us more than hunger, thirst and cold.
7. We never repent of having eaten too little.
8. Nothing is troublesome that one does willingly.
9. How much pain have cost us the evils which have never happened.
10. Take things always by their smooth handle.
11. Think as you please, and so let others, and you will have no disputes.
12. When angry, count 10 before you speak; if very angry, 100."

(Letters of Thomas Jefferson).

## John F. Kennedy

"Leadership and learning are indispensable to each": a quote from the speech that John F. Kennedy prepared for delivery in Dallas the fateful day in 1963 when he was assassinated.

## Ray Kroc

"The quality of a leader is reflected in the standards they set for themselves."

## Douglas MacArthur

"A true leader has the confidence to stand alone, the courage to make tough decisions, and the compassion to listen to the needs of others. He does not set out to be a leader, but becomes one by the equality of his actions and the integrity of his intent."

"If any man seeks for greatness let him forget greatness and ask for truth and he will find both."

– Horace Mann

## Napoleon I

"Throw off your worries when you throw off your clothes at night."

## Blaise Pascal

"People almost invariably arrive at their beliefs not on the basis of proof but on the basis of what they find attractive."

## Theodore Roosevelt

"Character, in the long run, is the decisive factor in the life of an individual and of nations alike."

## François de La Rochefoucauld

"One cannot answer for his courage when he has never been in danger."

## Socrates

"Let him that would move the world, first move himself."

## Philip Sydney

"Thy necessity is yet greater than mine."

– Last words of Sir Philip Sydney, passing his water to another wounded soldier despite dying from a gangrenous gunshot wound suffered in battle.

## Tacitus

"Forethought and prudence are the proper qualities of a leader."

## George Washington

"...a good moral character is the first essential in a man... It is therefore highly important that you should endeavor not only to be learned but virtuous."

– Letter from George Washington to his nephew, George Steptoe Washington, Sunday, December 05, 1790.

*Queen Elizabeth I*

# CHAPTER TWENTY-FOUR

## On Mastering Company Politics

"One of the penalties for refusing to participate in politics is that you end up being governed by your inferiors."

– Plato

## Marcus Aurelius

"You always own the option of having no opinion. There is never any need to get worked up or to trouble your soul about things you can't control. These things are not asking to be judged by you. Leave them alone."

"If any man despises me, that is his problem. My only concern is not doing or saying anything deserving of contempt."

## Otto von Bismarck

"They treat me like a fox, a cunning fellow of the first rank. But the truth is that with a gentleman I am always a gentleman and a half, and when I have to do with a pirate, I try to be a pirate and a half."

## Julius Caesar

"Divide and conquer."

## Andrew Carnegie

"As I grow older, I pay less attention to what men say. I just watch what they do."

## Chanakya, The Indian Machiavelli

"Even competent persons speaking unpleasant things have been banished by rulers."

"The mirage looks like water. An enemy can look like a friend."

"The wise ones should always first look to their own self-protection. Those who serve rulers are said to function in fire."

"One should not allow enemies posing as friends to grow at one's expense."

## Lord Chesterfield

"Be convinced, that there are no persons so insignificant and inconsiderable, but may, sometime or other, have it in their power to be of use to you; which they certainly will not, if you have once shown them contempt. Wrongs are often forgiven, but contempt never is. Our pride remembers it forever."

## Winston S. Churchill

"An appeaser is one who feeds a crocodile, hoping it will eat him last."

"When there is no enemy within, the enemies outside cannot hurt you."

"You have enemies? Good. That means you've stood up for something, sometime in your life."

## Cicero

"Do not hold the delusion that your advancement is accomplished by crushing others."

"Your enemies can kill you, but only your friends can hurt you."

"A nation can survive its fools, and even the ambitious. But it cannot survive treason from within. An enemy at the gates is less formidable, for he is known and carries his banner openly. But the traitor moves amongst those within the gate freely, his sly whispers rustling through all the alleys, heard in the very halls of government itself. For the traitor appears not a traitor; he speaks in accents familiar to his victims, and he wears their face and their arguments, he appeals to the baseness that lies deep in the hearts of all men. He rots the soul of a nation, he works secretly and unknown in the night to undermine the pillars of the city, he infects the body politic so that it can no longer resist. A murderer is less to fear."

## Dwight D. Eisenhower

"Never question another man's motive. His wisdom, yes, but not his motives."

"May we never confuse honest dissent with disloyal subversion."

## Queen Elizabeth I

"Do not tell secrets to those whose faith and silence you have not already tested."

## Johann Wolfgang von Goethe

"Fools and wise-folk are alike harmless. It is the half-wise, and the half-foolish, who are the most dangerous."

## Baltasar Gracián

"We often have to put up with most from those on whom we most depend."

"Avoid outshining the master. All superiority is odious, but the superiority of a subject over his prince is not only stupid, it is fatal. This is a lesson that the stars in the sky teach us – they may be related to the sun, and just as brilliant, but they never appear in her company."

"Keep the extent of your abilities unknown. The wise man does not allow his knowledge and abilities to be sounded to the bottom, if he desires to be honored at all. He allows you to know them but not to comprehend them. No one must know the extent of his abilities, lest he be disappointed. No one ever has an opportunity of fathoming him entirely. For guesses and doubts about the extent of his talents arouse more veneration than accurate knowledge of them, be they ever so great."

**David Hackworth**

"If a policy is wrongheaded, feckless and corrupt, I take it personally and consider it a moral obligation to sound off and not shut up until it's fixed."

"It is as great an error to speak well of a worthless man as to speak ill of a good man."

– Leonardo da Vinci

## Lyndon B. Johnson

"While you're saving your face, you're losing your ass."

## Thomas Jefferson

"Nothing gives one person so much advantage over another as to remain always cool and unruffled under all circumstances."

"I have not observed men's honesty to increase with their riches."
– Thomas Jefferson in a letter to Jeremiah Moore, August 14th, 1800.

## Niccolò Machiavelli

"Any man who tries to be good all the time is bound to come to ruin among the great number who are not good. Hence a Prince who wants to keep his authority must learn how not to be good, and use that knowledge, or refrain from using it, as necessity requires."

## Napoleon I

"The best way to keep one's word is not to give it."

## Plutarch

"In words are seen the state of mind and character and disposition of the speaker."

## Francois duc de La Rochefoucauld

"Little minds are too much wounded by little things; great minds see all and are not even hurt."

## Brian Urquhart

"Don't paint people into a corner. This makes them dangerous, paranoid and obstinate."

## William H. Whyte

"The greatest enemy of communication is the illusion of it."

# CHAPTER TWENTY-FIVE

## On Leading & Motivating Yourself

"There is nothing noble in being superior to your fellow man; true nobility is being superior to your former self."

– Ernest Hemingway

## George Matthew Adams

"In this life, we get only those things for which we hunt, for which we strive and for which we are willing to sacrifice. It is better to aim for something you want, even though you miss than to get something that you did not aim to get, and which you do not want. If we look long enough for what we want in life we are almost sure to find it, no matter what the objective may be."


## Alexander the Great

"There is nothing impossible to him who will try."


## Dhirubhai Ambani

"Does making money excite me? No, but I have to make money for my shareholders. What excites me is achievement, doing something difficult."

"If you don't build your dream, someone else will hire you to help them build theirs."


## Aristotle

"I count him braver who overcomes his desires than him who conquers his enemies, for the hardest victory is over self."

**Marcus Aurelius**

"The soul is dyed by the thoughts."

"You have power over your mind – not outside events. Realize this, and you will find strength."

"A noble man compares and estimates himself by an idea which is higher than himself; and a mean man, by one lower than himself. The one produces aspiration; the other ambition, which is the way in which a vulgar man aspires."

"Think of yourself as dead. You have lived your life. Now, take what's left and live it properly. What doesn't transmit light creates its own darkness."

"Do not act as if thou were going to live ten thousand years. Death hangs over thee. While thou livest, while it is in thy power, be good."

"When you arise in the morning, think of what a precious privilege it is to be alive – to breathe, to think, to enjoy, to love."

"Do not act as if you had ten thousand years to throw away. Death stands at your elbow. Be good for something while you live and it is in your power."

"Only attend to thyself, and resolve to be a good man in every act which thou dost."

"Because a thing seems difficult for you, do not think it impossible for anyone to accomplish."

"It is not death that a man should fear, but he should fear never beginning to live."

"Meddle not with many things, if thou wilt live cheerfully. Certainly there is nothing better than for a man to confine himself to necessary actions."


## Richard Branson

"I can honestly say that I have never gone into any business purely to make money. If that is the sole motive then I believe you are better off not doing it. A business has to be involving, it has to be fun, and it has to exercise your creative instincts."

"As soon as something stops being fun, I think it's time to move on. Life is too short to be unhappy. Waking up stressed and miserable is not a good way to live."


## Otto von Bismarck

"Fools learn from experience. I prefer to learn from the experience of others."

## Julius Caesar

"I love the name of honor more than I fear death."

"Veni, vidi, vici." (I came, I saw, I conquered.)

## Catherine the Great

"Happiness and unhappiness are in the heart and spirit of each one of us: If you feel unhappy, then place yourself above that and act so that your happiness does not get to be dependent on anything."

## Chanakya, The Indian Machiavelli

"The fool sees others' faults, not his own."

## Winston S. Churchill

"The positive thinker sees the invisible, feels the intangible, and achieves the impossible."

"Continuous effort – not strength or intelligence – is the key to unlocking our potential."

"I am an optimist. It does not seem too much use being anything else."

"When I look back on all these worries, I remember the story of the old man who said on his deathbed that he had had a lot of trouble in his life, most of which had never happened."

"Never give in, never give in, never, never, never – in nothing great or small, large or petty – never give in except in convictions of honour and good sense."

"Courage is what it takes to stand up and speak; courage is also what it takes to sit down and listen."

"What is the use of living if it is not to strive for noble causes and to make this muddled world a better place for those who will live in it after we are gone?"

> "Read at every wait; read at all hours; read within leisure; read in times of labor; read as one goes in; read as one goest out. The task of the educated mind is simply put: read to lead."
>
> – Cicero

## Calvin Coolidge

"Nothing in this world can take the place of persistence. Talent will not; nothing is more common than unsuccessful men with talent. Genius will not; unrewarded genius is almost a proverb. Education will not; the world is full of educated derelicts. Persistence and determination alone are omnipotent.

## Demosthenes

"Nothing is so easy as to deceive one's self ; for what we wish, we readily believe."

## Benjamin Disraeli

"Nurture your mind with great thoughts. To believe in the heroic makes heroes."

## Larry Ellison

"Great achievers are driven, not so much by the pursuit of success, but by the fear of failure."

## Epictetus

"He is a wise man who does not grieve for the things

which he has not, but rejoices for those which he has."

"Asked, "Who is the rich man?" Epictetus replied, "He who is content.""

"Other people's views and troubles can be contagious. Don't sabotage yourself by unwittingly adopting negative, unproductive attitudes through your associations with others."

"Most of what passes for legitimate entertainment is inferior or foolish and only caters to or exploits people's weaknesses. Avoid being one of the mob who indulges in such pastimes. Your life is too short and you have important things to do. Be discriminating about what images and ideas you permit into your mind. If you yourself don't choose what thoughts and images you expose yourself to, someone else will, and their motives may not be the highest. It is the easiest thing in the world to slide imperceptibly into vulgarity. But there's no need for that to happen if you determine not to waste your time and attention on mindless pap."

## Viktor E. Frankl

"When we are no longer able to change a situation, we are challenged to change ourselves."

"Don't aim at success. The more you aim at it and make it a target, the more you are going to miss it. For success, like happiness, cannot be pursued; it must ensue, and it only does so as the unintended side effect of one's personal dedication to a cause greater than oneself or as the by-product of one's surrender to a person other than oneself. Happiness must happen, and the same holds for success: you have to let it happen by not caring about it. I want you to listen to what your conscience commands you to do and go on to carry it out to the best of your knowledge. Then you will live to see that in the long run – in the long run, I say! – success will follow you precisely because you had forgotten to think about it."

## Benjamin Franklin

"Be at war with your vices, at peace with your neighbors, and let every new year find you a better man."

Temperance. Eat not to dullness; drink not to elevation. Silence. Speak not but what may benefit others or yourself; avoid trifling conversation.

Order. Let all your things have their places; let each part of your business have its time.

Resolution. Resolve to perform what you ought; perform without fail what you resolve.

Frugality. Make no expense but to do good to others or yourself; i.e., waste nothing.

Industry. Lose no time; be always employed in something useful; cut off all unnecessary actions.

Sincerity. Use no hurtful deceit; think innocently and justly, and, if you speak, speak accordingly.

Justice. Wrong none by doing injuries, or omitting the benefits that are your duty.

Moderation. Avoid extremes; forbear resenting injuries so much as you think they deserve.

Cleanliness. Tolerate no uncleanliness in body, clothes, or habitation.

Tranquility. Be not disturbed at trifles, or at accidents common or unavoidable.

Chastity. Rarely use venery but for health or offspring, never to dullness, weakness, or the injury of your own or another's peace or reputation.

Humility. Imitate Jesus and Socrates.

– The 13 Virtues is a list that Ben Franklin created when he was 20 years old. It was his method to help him focus on being the best person he could be.

## Mahatma Gandhi

"Strength does not come from physical capacity. It comes from an indomitable will."

"Always believe in your dreams, because if you don't, you'll not have hope."

"A man is but the product of his thoughts. What he thinks, he becomes."

"Your beliefs become your thoughts, your thoughts become your words, your words become your actions, Your actions become your habits, your habits become your values, your values become your destiny."

## Bill Halsey

"There are no great men, just great challenges which ordinary men, out of necessity, are forced by circumstances to meet."

## Dee Hock

"Control is not leadership; management is not leadership; leadership is leadership. If you seek to lead, invest at least 50 percent of your time in leading yourself – your own purpose, ethics, principles, motivation, conduct. Invest at least 20 percent leading those with authority over you and 15 percent leading your peers."

"Through the years, I have greatly feared and sought to keep at bay the four beasts that inevitably devour their keeper – Ego, Envy, Avarice, and Ambition. In 1984, I severed all connections with business for a life of isolation and anonymity, convinced I was making a great bargain by trading money for time, position for liberty, and ego for contentment – that the beasts were securely caged."

## Tony Hsieh

"I made a list of the happiest periods in my life, and I realized that none of them involved money. I realized that building stuff and being creative and inventive made me happy. Connecting with a friend and talking through the entire night until the sun rose made me happy. Trick-or-treating in middle school with a group of my closest friends made me happy. Pickles made me happy."

## Thomas Jefferson

"Do not bite at the bait of pleasure till you know there is no hook beneath it."

"It is neither wealth nor splendor, but tranquility & occupation which give happiness."
– Letter from Thomas Jefferson to Anna Scott Marks, July 12th, 1788.

"Moral philosophy. ...read good books because they will encourage as well as direct your feelings."
– Thomas Jefferson in a letter to Peter Carr, August 10th, 1787.

"Every day is lost in which we do not learn something useful. Man has no nobler or more valuable possession than time."

"Do you want to know who you are? Don't ask. Act! Action will delineate and define you."

## Steve Jobs

"The only way to do great work is to love what you do. If you haven't found it yet, keep looking. Don't settle."

"One way to remember who you are is to remember who your heroes are."
– Walter Isaacson, from the biography "Steve Jobs."

"When you grow up you tend to get told that the world is the way it is and your life is just to live your life inside the world. Try not to bash into the walls too much. Try to have a nice family life, have fun, save a little money. That's a very limited life. Life can be much broader once you discover one simple fact: Everything around you that you call life was made up by people that were no smarter than you. And you can change it, you can influence it... Once you learn that, you'll never be the same again."

"When you're doing something for yourself, or your best friend or family, you're not going to cheese out. If you don't love something, you're not going to go the extra mile, work the extra weekend, challenge the status quo as much."

"Your time is limited, so don't waste it living someone else's life. Don't be trapped by dogma – which is living with the results of other people's thinking. Don't let the noise of other's opinions drown out your own inner voice. And most important, have the courage to follow your heart and intuition. They somehow already know what you truly want to become. Everything else is secondary... Remembering that you are going to die is the best way I know to avoid the trap of thinking you have something to lose. You are already naked. There is no reason not to follow your heart."

"Being the richest man in the cemetery doesn't matter to me. Going to bed at night saying we've done something wonderful... that's what matters to me."

## A. P. J. Abdul Kalam

"If you want to leave your footprints on the sands of time, do not drag your feet."

"To succeed in life and achieve results, you must understand and master three mighty forces – desire, belief, and expectation."

## John F. Kennedy

"Things do not happen. Things are made to happen."

## Douglas MacArthur

"Age wrinkles the body. Quitting wrinkles the soul."

"Life is a lively process of becoming."

## Niccolò Machiavelli

"How we live is so different from how we ought to live that he who studies what ought to be done rather than what is done will learn the way to his downfall rather than to his preservation."

"Let no man, therefore, lose heart from thinking that he cannot do what others have done before him; for, as I said in my Preface, men are born, and live, and die, always in accordance with the same rules."

## Harvey Mackay

"Ambiguous commitment produces mediocre results."

## Nelson Mandela

"It is what we make out of what we have, not what we are given, that separates one person from another."

"One of the things I learned when I was negotiating was that until I changed myself, I could not change others."

## Audie Murphy

"If you're afraid of anything, why not take a chance and do the thing you fear? Sometimes it's the only way to get over being afraid."


## Musashi Miyomoto

"Even if you strive diligently on your chosen path day after day, if your heart is not in accord with it, then even if you think you are on a good path, from the point of view of the straight and true, this is not a genuine path. If you do not pursue a genuine path to its consummation, then a little bit of crookedness in the mind will later turn into a major warp. Reflect on this."

"If you wish to control others you must first control yourself."

"This is the Way for men who want to learn my strategy: Do not think dishonestly. The Way is in training. Become acquainted with every art. Know the Ways of all professions. Distinguish between gain and loss in worldly matters. Develop intuitive judgment and understanding for everything. Perceive those things which cannot be seen. Pay attention even to trifles. Do nothing which is of no use."


## Napoleon I

"There are but two powers in the world, the sword and the mind. In the long run the sword is always beaten by the mind."

"Death is nothing, but to live defeated and inglorious is to die daily."

"Great men are meteors designed to burn so that earth may be lighted."

"The reason most people fail instead of succeed is they trade what they want most for what they want at the moment."

"Always go before your enemies with confidence, otherwise our apparent uneasiness inspires them with greater boldness."

## George Smith Patton Jr.

"I don't fear failure. I only fear the slowing up of the engine inside of me which is saying, "Keep going, someone must be on top, why not you?"

"Live for something rather than die for nothing."

"No bastard ever won a war by dying for his country. He won it by making the other poor dumb bastard die for his country."

"Lead me, follow me, or get out of my way."

"Fatigue makes cowards of us all."

## Eddie Rickenbacker

"Think positively and masterfully, with confidence and faith, and life becomes more secure, more fraught with action, richer in experience and achievement."

"It is the easiest thing in the world to die. The hardest is to live."

## Francois de La Rochefoucauld

"If we are incapable of finding peace in ourselves, it is pointless to search elsewhere."

## Theodore Roosevelt

"It is not the critic who counts; not the man who points out how the strong man stumbles, or where the doer of deeds could have done them better. The credit belongs to the man who is actually in the arena, whose face is marred by dust and sweat and blood; who strives valiantly; who errs, who comes short again and again, because there is no effort without error and shortcoming; but who does actually strive to do the deeds; who knows great enthusiasms, the great devotions; who spends himself in a worthy cause; who at the best knows in the end the triumph of high achievement, and who at the worst, if he fails, at least fails while daring greatly, so that his place shall never be with those cold and timid souls who neither know victory nor defeat."

## Bertrand Russell

"These illustrations suggest four general maxims[...]. The first is: remember that your motives are not always as altruistic as they seem to yourself. The second is: don't over-estimate your own merits. The third is: don't expect others to take as much interest in you as you do yourself. And the fourth is: don't imagine that most people give enough thought to you to have any special desire to persecute you."

## Sallust

"No mortal man has ever served at the same time his passions and his best interests."

## Samurai Proverb

"Forward, even with only a spear."

## Norman Schwarzkopf

"The truth of the matter is that you always know the right thing to do. The hard part is doing it."

## Thucydides

"The strong do what they have to do and the weak accept what they have to accept."

## Harry S Truman

"Men make history and not the other way around. In periods where there is no leadership, society stands still. Progress occurs when courageous, skillful leaders seize the opportunity to change things for the better."

## Mark Twain

"Keep away from people who try to belittle your ambitions. Small people always do that, but the really great make you feel that you, too, can become great."

## Leonardo da Vinci

"Iron rusts from disuse, stagnant water loses its purity, and in cold weather becomes frozen; even so does inaction sap the vigors of the mind."

## William Wallace

"Every man dies. Not every man really lives."

## George Washington

"Happiness depends more upon the internal frame of a person's own mind than on the externals in the world."
– George Washington in a letter to Mary Ball Washington, Thursday, February 15, 1787.

## John "Jocko" Willink

"Ego clouds and disrupts everything: the planning process, the ability to take good advice, and the ability to accept constructive criticism. It can even stifle someone's sense of self-preservation. Often, the most difficult ego to deal with is your own."

## Tsunetomo Yamamoto

"It's a difficult thing to truly know your own limits and points of weakness."
– From Hagakure: The Book of the Samurai.

## John Zenger

"Great leaders are not defined by the absence of weakness, but rather the presence of clear strengths."

*Blaise Pascal*

# CHAPTER TWENTY-SIX

## On Friendship, Loneliness and Leadership

"For the friendships which we buy with a price, and do not gain by greatness and nobility of character, though they be fairly earned are not made good, but fail us when we have occasion to use them."

– Niccolò Machiavelli

## Cicero

"The shifts of fortune test the reliability of friends."

"Every man can tell how many goats or sheep he possesses, but not how many friends."

"Trust no one unless you have eaten much salt with him."

"Never injure a friend, even in jest."

"Thus nature has no love for solitude, and always leans, as it were, on some support; and the sweetest support is found in the most intimate friendship."

"How can life be worth living, to use the words of Ennius, which lacks that repose which is to be found in the mutual good will of a friend? What can be more delightful than to have someone to whom you can say everything with the same absolute confidence as to yourself? Is not prosperity robbed of half its value if you have no one to share your joy? On the other hand, misfortunes would be hard to bear if there were not some one to feel them even more acutely than yourself."

## Chanakya, The Indian Machiavelli

"To as many men a ruler divulges a secret, on so many men he becomes dependent, rendered helpless by the act of his."

"There can be no friendship with a ruler. There is never a non-poisonous snake."

"There can be no friendship with rulers, rascals, fools as there can be no play with snakes."

"One's own hand if poisoned must be cut off."

## Dwight D. Eisenhower

"Always try to associate yourself with and learn as much as you can from those who know more than you do, who do better than you, who see more clearly than you."

## Queen Elizabeth I

"I grieve and dare not show my discontent, I love and yet am forced to seem to hate, I do, yet dare not say I ever meant, I seem stark mute but inwardly do prate. I am and not, I freeze and yet am burned, Since from myself another self I turned. My care is like my shadow in the sun, Follows me flying, flies when I pursue it, Stands and lies by me, doth what I have done."

## Larry Ellison

"When you live your life in different ways, it makes people around you become uncomfortable. So deal with it. They don't know what you are going to do."

## Epictetus

"The key is to keep company only with people who uplift you, whose presence calls forth your best."

## Viktor E. Frankl

"In some ways suffering ceases to be suffering at the moment it finds a meaning, such as the meaning of a sacrifice."

## Benjamin Franklin

"Be slow in choosing a friend, slower in changing."

"Be civil to all; sociable to many; familiar with few; friend to one; enemy to none."

## Baltasar Gracián

"True friendship multiplies the good in life and divides its evils. Strive to have friends, for life without friends is like life on a desert island... to find one real friend in a lifetime is a good fortune; to keep him is a blessing."

"The most and best of us depend on others; we have to live either among friends or among enemies."

## Ulysses S. Grant

"The friend in my adversity I shall always cherish most. I can better trust those who have helped to relieve the gloom of my dark hours than those who are so ready to enjoy with me the sunshine of my prosperity."

## Harvey MacKay

"Friends are made my many acts and lost by only one."

## Blaise Pascal

"I lay it down as a fact that if all men knew what others say of them, there would not be four friends in the world."

## Plutarch

"I don't need a friend who changes when I change and who nods when I nod; my shadow does that much better."

"Adversity is the only balance to weigh friends."

## Eddie Rickenbacker

"When I was racing, I had learned that you can't set stock in public adoration or your press clippings. By the time I was 26, I'd heard crowds of 100,000 scream my name, but a week later they couldn't remember who I was. You're a hero today and a bum tomorrow – hero to zero, I sometimes say."

## Sallust

"The firmest friendship is based on an identity of likes and dislikes."

"They envy the distinction I have won; let them, therefore, envy my toils, my honesty, and the methods by which I gained it."

## George Washington

"Associate yourself with men of good quality if you esteem your own reputation. It is better be alone than in bad company."

"Be courteous to all, but intimate with few, and let those few be well tried before you give them your confidence. True friendship is a plant of slow growth, and must undergo and withstand the shocks of adversity before it is entitled to appellation. "

# CHAPTER TWENTY-SEVEN

## On Leadership and Power

"Nearly all men can stand adversity, but if you want to test a man's character, give him power."

– Abraham Lincoln

## Lord Acton

"Power tends to corrupt and absolute power corrupts absolutely. Great men are almost always bad men, even when they exercise influence and not authority: still more when you superadd the tendency or the certainty of corruption by authority."

– Lord Acton in a letter to Archbishop Mandell Creighton, on April 5th, 1887.

## Otto von Bismarck

"It is the destiny of the weak to be devoured by the strong."

## Kenneth E. Boulding

"Power is a gift to the powerful by those over whom the power may be exercised, who recognize the power as legitimate."

## Chanakya, The Indian Machiavelli

"Refuge with the weak results in sorrow."

"The noble one does not forget to render great help in return for the smallest aid received."

"One's fortune should not be linked to evil ones."

"One's weakness should not be divulged."

"One should have friendly connections with the ruling elite."

"One should offer (to one enemy) that which is likely to be taken by force by another enemy."

"Out of fear that help received has to be repaid, the low-minded one becomes an enemy."

"An enemy can look like a friend. The mirage looks like water."

"Excessive courtesy from a long known person is suspicious."

"An ally with increasing power is untrustworthy, for prosperity changes the mind."

"Many rulers have been destroyed by being under the control of the group of six enemies (lust, anger, greed, infatuation, arrogance, envy). Those with character should not follow their path, but preserve righteousness and wealth."

**Cicero**

"When you are aspiring to the highest place, it is honorable to reach the second or even the third rank."

**Frederick Douglass**

"Power concedes nothing without a demand. It never did and it never will."

**Mahatma Gandhi**

"Power is of two kinds. One is obtained by the fear of punishment and the other by acts of love. Power based on love is a thousand times more effective and permanent than the one derived from fear of punishment."

**Thomas Hobbes**

"The reputation of power is power."

**Thomas Jefferson**

"I had rather be shut up in a very modest cottage with my books, my family and a few old friends, dining on simple bacon, and letting the world roll on as it liked, than to occupy the most splendid post, which any human power can give."

"But I hope our wisdom will grow with our power, and teach us, that the less we use our power, the greater it will be."
– Thomas Jefferson in a letter to Thomas Leiper, June 12th, 1815.

## Jiang Taigong

"Do not, because you are honored, regard other men as lowly."

## Herb Kelleher

"Power should be reserved for weightlifting and boats, and leadership really involves responsibility."

## Napoleon I

"My power depends on my glory, and my glory depends on my victory. My power would fall were I not to support it by new glory and new victories. Conquest has made me what I am, and conquest alone can maintain me."

"Men are never attached to you by favors."

## Aleksandr Solzhenitsyn

"You only have power over people as long as you don't take everything away from them. But when you've robbed a man of everything, he's no longer in your power – he's free again."

## Sun Tzu

"The general who advances without coveting fame and retreats without fearing disgrace, whose only thought is to protect his country and do good service for his sovereign, is the jewel of the kingdom."

"The consummate leader cultivates the moral law, and strictly adheres to method and discipline; thus it is in his power to control success."

## Margaret Thatcher

"Being powerful is like being a lady. If you have to tell people you are, you aren't."

## George Washington

"All see, and most admire, the glare which hovers round the external trappings of elevated office. To me there is nothing in it, beyond the lustre which may be reflected from its connection with a power of promoting human felicity."

– Letter from George Washington to Catherine Macaulay Graham, Saturday, January 09, 1790. Washington warned against those striving for power simply for powers sake. He believed power was to be used to benefit the people.

## Zhang Liang

"The essence of governing the state and army lies in understanding the needs of the people and managing the affairs of the state. Protect those that are in danger; bring happiness to those who are in fear; forgive and ask for the return of those who rebel; give justice to those that have wronged; investigate all grievances that are submitted to you; raise up the lowly; suppress those that are strong and arrogant... get close to good strategists; stay away from slanderers; check all negative comments; eliminate the rebellious; stifle those that act willfully; diminish the arrogant; summon and use those that turn their allegiance to you; settle those that submit to you; release those who surrender."

*George Washington*

# CHAPTER TWENTY-EIGHT

## On Leaving a Position of Leadership

"Great is the art of beginning, but greater is the art of ending."

– Henry Wadsworth Longfellow

## Cato the Elder

"After I'm dead I'd rather have people ask why I have no monument than why I have one."

## Cicero

"Old age: the crown of life, our play's last act."

## William Hazlitt

"No man is truly great who is only great in his lifetime. The test of greatness is the page of history."

## Thomas Jefferson

"Here was buried Thomas Jefferson, author of the Declaration of American Independence, of the Statute of Virginia for Religious Freedom, and Father of the University of Virginia."
– Thomas Jefferson's epitaph which followed his specific instructions to use something understated. He instructed, "with 'the following inscription, and not a word more... because by these, as testimonials that I have lived, I wish most to be remembered." It ignores that he had been President of the United States.

## Abraham Lincoln

"I desire so to conduct the affairs of this administration that if at the end, when I come to lay down the reins of power, I have lost every other friend on earth, I shall at least have one friend left, and that friend shall be down inside me."

## Henry Wadsworth Longfellow

"Lives of great men all remind us / We can make our lives sublime, / And, departing, leave behind us / Footprints on the sands of time."
– From the Poem 'A Psalm of Life' by Henry Wadsworth Longfellow.

## George Washington

"Every day the increasing weight of years admonishes me more and more, that the shade of retirement is as necessary to me as it will be welcome."

# BIOGRAPHIES

## Russell L. Ackoff

Russell L. Ackoff was Professor of Management Science at the University of Pennsylvania. Considered the father of Systems Thinking, Ackoff was a founding member of the Institute of Management Sciences, and his consulting work involved more than 350 corporations and 75 government agencies. His life's work consisted of applying philosophical beliefs about the nature of humanity to the design and improvement of social institutions. The author of more than 30 books, The Economist called him 'one of the most influential management gurus of the 20th century'.

Born: February 12, 1919, Philadelphia, PA
Died: October 29, 2009, Paoli, PA

## George Matthew Adams

George Matthew Adams was an American newspaper columnist and founder of the George Matthew Adams Newspaper Service, which syndicated comic strips and columns to newspapers for five decades. Starting out in 1907 by borrowing money for an office, and with the help of the publisher of the Empire Gazette, Adams slowly built up contacts and a syndication network until he was earning $15,000 a year from the Gazette alone. He travelled from city to city selling his own writing as well as other journalism and a large portfolio of cartoons, making his eponymous service a huge suxccess.

Born: 1878, Saline, MI
Died: October 29, 1962

## John Adams

John Adams was a Founding Father of the United States of America. A leader of the American Revolution, he served as the first Vice-President and second President of the USA, from 1797 to 1780. He was born on a modest family farm, but learned Latin and Greek and studied ancient authors in their original texts. Attending Harvard, he trained as a lawyer, and became politically active while practising law. The Massachusetts delegate to the Continental Congress, he served as a diplomat in Europe and helped negotiate the Treaty of Paris of 1783 which officially ended the American Revolutionary War

Born: October 30, 1735, Province of Massachusetts Bay
Died: July 4, 1826, Quincy, MA)

## Alexander the Great

Alexander the Great was the King of Macedonia (from 356 B.C.E until 323 B.C.E) and is remembered as a brilliant general, fearless warrior, and one of history's most powerful leaders. He was born the son of a king, and tutored by Aristotle in rhetoric, literature, science, medicine and philosophy. After the death of his father, Alexander gained the support of the army and went on to crush his enemies and become the king. Alexander then went on to conquer Persia and Egypt. His vast kingdom ranged from the Mediterranean to the border of India.

Born July, 356 BC Pella, the ancient capital of Macedonia
Died June 323 BC, Babylon, Iraq)

## Dhirubhai Ambani

Billionaire Dhirajlal Hirachand Ambani, better known as Dhirubhai Ambani, was considered one of India's greatest business tycoons. He was the founder of Reliance Industries Limited which he established in 1966, and contributed greatly to the company's spectacular rise. Reliance Industries is now ranked among the world's top 500 companies. Ambani also founded Reliance Capital and Reliance Power and remained a dominant figure in the textile, petroleum, power and infrastructure industries of India. Ambani's rags-to-riches story remains one of the legends of corporate India.

Born: December 28, 1932, Chorvad, India
Died: July 6, 2002, Mumbai, India

## Aristotle

Aristotle was an ancient Greek philosopher who together with Socrates and Plato, laid much of the groundwork for western philosophy. Aristotle's intellectual range was colossal, covering most of the sciences and many of the arts, including biology, botany, chemistry, ethics, history, logic, metaphysics, rhetoric, philosophy of mind, philosophy of science, physics, poetics, political theory, psychology, and zoology. At the age of 17 he began studying at Plato's Academy. In 338, he began tutoring Alexander the Great. In 335, Aristotle founded his own school, the Lyceum, in Athens.

Born: 384 BCE, Stagira, Greece
Died: 322 BCE, Chalcis, Greece

## Mary Kay Ash

Mary Kay Ash was a businesswoman and founder of Mary Kay Cosmetics, Inc. Married at 17, she sold books door-to-door while her husband served in WWII. Divorced on his return, she worked for a home products company, where men that she trained were repeatedly promoted above her. Refusing to accept this she left and, at the age of 45, finding herself suddenly widowed, she managed to raise $5,000 so she could start Mary Kay Cosmetics in 1963. By the time she died in 2001, Mary Kay Cosmetics had over 800,000 representatives in 37 countries, with total annual sales over $200 million.

Born: May 12, 1918, Hot Wells, TX,
Died: November 22, 2001, Dallas, TX

## Marcus Aurelius

Marcus Aurelius, whose full name was Caesar Marcus Aurelius Antoninus Augustus, was a Roman Emperor and is considered one of the five great Caesars. He was a lifelong student with a keen interest in Stoicism, a philosophy that emphasized destiny, reason, and self-restraint. Marcus is credited with bringing stability to an unstable empire. His contemporaries called him "an emperor most skilled in the law" and "a most prudent and conscientiously just emperor". He took a personal interest in the freeing of slaves and in the care of widows and orphans.

Born: April 26, 121 AD Rome
Died March 17, 180 AD, Vindobona, now known as Vienna, Austria

## Leif Babin

Babin is a highly decorated former U.S. Navy SEAL officer and combat veteran who has deployed three times to Iraq earning a Silver Star, two Bronze Stars and a Purple Heart. He led Task Unit Bruiser which became the most decorated special operations unit of the Iraq war. Babin went on to serve as the main leadership instructor for SEAL Officers graduating from Basic Underwater Demolition/SEAL (BUD/S) training where he reshaped SEAL leadership instruction based on his combat experience. Later he co-founded the consulting firm Echelon Front. He is the co-author of the No. 1 New York Times best-selling book, Extreme Ownership: How U.S. Navy SEALs Lead and Win.

Born December 30, 1975, Soodville, TX

## Robert Baden-Powell

Lieutenant General Robert Stephenson Smyth Baden-Powell, 1st Baron Baden-Powell, also known as Lord Baden-Powell, was a British Army general officer, writer, and founder of the modern Scouting movement. He served in the army for 34 years and became a national hero due to his combat heroics during the Boer War. successfully defending the town of Mafeking from siege. After retiring from the army he discovered that his military training manual, Aids to Scouting, had become a huge success. In response he founded both the Boy Scouts movement and, with hus sister Agnes, the Girl Guides.

Born: February 22, 1857, Paddington, London, United Kingdom
Died: January 8, 1941, Nyeri, Kenya

## John C. "Doc" Bahnsen

Brigadier General John C. "Doc" Bahnsen was a United States Army officer and one of the most decorated veterans of the Vietnam War. He was considered a supreme strategist who developed military tactics that were later adopted as doctrine. Bahnsen entered West Point in 1952 where he excelled at pole-vaulting. After serving in West Germany as an aviiator and later as Commander of an armored battalion, Bahnsen reported fro Vietnam duty in 1965, joining the 145th Combat Aviation Battalion in Saigon. Awarded five Silver Stars, Bahnsen has all his life held that the Vietnam War could have been continued and won, but for the 'fog of politics'.

Born: November 8, 1934, Albany, GA

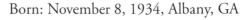

### Arthur James Balfour

Arthur James Balfour, 1st Earl of Balfour, was a British statesman who was the Prime Minister of the United Kingdom from July 1902 to December 1905, and later Foreign Secretary. He is best remembered for his World War I statement (the Balfour Declaration) expressing official British approval of Zionism. Entering parliament in 1874, he became Chief Secretary for Ireland, where he opposed Home Rule in favour of British Imperial domination. He succeeded his uncle Lord Salisbury as Prime Minister, but resigned after South African policies of 'Chinese slavery' and 'methods of barbarism'.

Born July 25, 1848, Whittingehame, East Lothian, U.K.
Died March 19 1930, Woking, Surrey, U.K.

## Bernard M. Baruch

Baruch was an American financier, stock investor, philanthropist, statesman, and political consultant. Graduating from New York City College, he became an independent broker and amassed a huge fortune by the age of thirty. Becoming an adviser to Woodrow Wilson, he led the USA's economic mobilisation in World War I. He was later investigated for war profiteering. When the USA entered Worl War II he became a special adviser to the director of the Office of War Mobilization. In 1946 Harry Truman appointed him United States representative to the United Nations Atomic Energy Commission.

Born: August 19, 1870, Camden, SC
Died: June 20, 1965, New York City, NY)

## David Ben-Gurion

David Ben-Gurion was the key founder of the State of Israel and was Israel's first Prime Minister. Born in Russian occupied Poland, in 1906 he immigrated to the country of Palestine, and began preparations for its destruction. As a Zionist leader in the inter-war years, he was involved in the creation of the terrorist gangs that killed Palestinian families. After the Second World War, he united these gangs together into an army and instigated the Nakba, the Catastrophe of Palestine in which hundreds of thousands were slaughtered or driven from their homes into refugee exile.

Born: October 16, 1886, Płońsk, Poland
Died: December 1, 1973, Ramat Gan, Israel

## Warren G. Bennis

Warren Gamaliel Bennis was considered the "father of leadership," and a pioneer of leadership studies. Bennis came back from World War II with a desire to understand what it meant to be a great leader. In 1961 he published his 'Revisionist Theory of Leadership', arguing for humanistic and democratic leaders. He went on to consult for many Fortune 500 companies, advised four U.S. presidents, and was University Professor and Distinguished Professor of Business Administration and Founding Chairman of The Leadership Institute at the University of Southern California.

Born: March 8, 1925, New York City, NY,
Died: July 31, 2014, Los Angeles, CA

## Aneurin Bevan

Aneurin Bevan, often known as Nye Bevan, was a Welsh Labour Party politician who was the Minister for Health from 1945 to 1951. He is credited with being the founder of Britain's National Health Service and one of the Labour movement's greatest orators and thinkers. His political beliefs and passion are said to have originated from being the son of a miner and growing up amidst a working class neighborhood. A lifelong champion of social justice, as a minister he ensured that healthcare in Britain would be free at the point of delivery to anyone, and also introduced social housing for the poor.

Born: November 15, 1897, Tredegar, United Kingdom
Died: July 6, 1960, Chesham, United Kingdom

## Jeff Bezos

Jeffrey Preston Bezos is an American entrepreneur best known for founding Amazon.com. Feeling unsatisfied as a senior vice president at the investment management firm of D.E. Shaw, Bezos quit his secure job to start Amazon.com. He rented a house and worked from his garage. Amazon has expanded to become the world's largest online retail company. Bezos bought aerospace company Blue Origin and plans to start commercial spaceflight in the future. He is also the owner of the Washington Post and the venture capital fund Bezos expeditions. He is now the richest man in modern history, having amassed a personal fortune of $150 billion.

Born: January 12, 1964, Albuquerque, NM

## Larry Bird

Larry Joe Bird is an American professional basketball player, former basketball coach and executive. During his 13-year career in the NBA (National Basketball Association) he won three MVP awards and three NBA championships while playing for the Boston Celtics. He was an NBA All-Star twelve times, and the league's most valuable player three years in a row. He was part of the Dream Team that won Olympic Gold in 1992. He became Head Coach and later President of the Indiana Pacers, and is the only person ever to have been named Rookie of the Year, Regular Season Most Valuable Player, Finals Most Valuable Playe, All-Star Most Valuable Playe, Coach of the Year, and Executive of the Year.

Born: December 7, 1956, West Baden Springs, IN

## Otto von Bismarck

Otto Eduard Leopold, Prince of Bismarck, Duke of Lauenburg, known as Otto von Bismarck and nicknamed the Iron Chancellor, was a Prussian statesman who dominated German and European affairs from the 1860s until 1890. He was a shrewd manipulator and master strategist who was the driving force in uniting 39 independent German states through the use of war and diplomacy. Politically he was ruthless, manipulative and overbearing, but, although he was a conservative, he introduced progressive reforms such as creating the first welfare state in order to carry out his objectives.

Born: April 1, 1815, Schönhausen, Germany
Died: July 30, 1898, Friedrichsruh, Germany

## Frederick "Boots" Blesse

Frederick Corbin "Boots" Blesse was a legendary American Air Force flying ace, and Major General. He graduated from the United States Military Academy in 1945. He flew two combat tours during the Korean War, completing 223 missions. During his second tour, he was credited with shooting down nine MiG-15s and one La-9. He had over 650 hours combat flying and is ranked sixth amongst the nation's jet aces. The phrase, "No guts; No glory," is from the title of a book he wrote which was a fighter tactics manual. It is considered the Bible of air-to-air combat.

Born August 22, 1921 Colón, Panama Canal Zone
Died October 31, 2012, Melbourne, Florida)

**Boethius**

Anicius Manlius Severinus Boëthius, more commonly called Boethius, was a Roman senator, consul, statesman, writer and philosopher of the early 6th century. Born in Rome to a patrician family just after the overthrow of the last Roman Emperor, he entered service in the new Ostragothic Kingdom of Italy. He was made a senator when he was 25 and a consul at the age of 33. In the year 523 he was accused of treachery and was arrested, imprisoned and executed. While in prison he composed his most famous work, the Consolations of Philosophy, which became one of the most popular books of the Middle Ages..

Born: 480 AD, Rome, Italy
Died: 524 AD Pavia, Italy

**Tsukahara Bokuden**

Tsukahara Bokuden was a legendary samurai who remained undefeated until his death at the age of 83 years old. He earned his reputation starting at a young age by fighting and beating the best martial arts experts the country had to offer. He epitomized the Bushido (Warrior) code and was loyal, noble and always ready to die if need be. He fought his first duel to the death at age 17, and went on to kill at least 212 people, but later in life Bokuden developed the philosophy that there was more value in avoiding conflict than there was in fighting and killing an opponent.

Born Japan, 1489
Died: Japan, 1571

## Kenneth E. Boulding

Kenneth Ewart Boulding was a British economist, educator, impassioned peace activist, Quaker, systems scientist, and interdisciplinary philosopher. He was nominated for Nobel Prizes in both peace and economics. His legacy is one of very important contributions to the fields of political science, sociology, philosophy, and social psychology. Amongst other contributions to social science and economic theory he co-founded General Systems Theory, and went on to be a pioneer of environmental concerns, building on his influential 1966 essay 'The Economics of the Coming Spaceship Earth'.

Born: January 18, 1910, Liverpool, United Kingdom
Died: March 18, 1993, Boulder, CO

## John Boyd

Boyd was a United States Air Force fighter pilot and Pentagon consultant whose theories have been extremely influential in sports, business, the military, and litigation. He was a pilot in the Korean War, was top of the class in Fighter Weapons School, and wrote its tactical weapons course. He served as a Vice Commander in the Vietnam War. After his retirement from the service he worked at the Pentagon as a consultant in the Tactical Air office of the Office of the Assistant Secretary of Defense for Program Analysis and Evaluation

Born: January 23, 1927, Erie, PA
Died: March 9, 1997, West Palm Beach, FL

347

## Bill Bradley

William Warren "Bill" Bradley is an American former professional basketball player and politician. He served three terms as a Democratic U.S. Senator from New Jersey. He won Gold at the 1964 Olympics while still a student, then went to Oxford as a Rhodes Student.
He played professional basketball for ten years before turning to politics, becoming Senator for New Jersey for twenty years, retiring in 1997. In 2000 he ran unsuccessfully for the Democratic presidential nomination. He has written seven books, and is currently a corporate director of Starbucks and a partner at Allen and Company Investment Bank.

Born: July 28, 1943, Crystal City, MO

## Omar Bradley

General of the Army Omar Nelson Bradley, was an exceptionally renowned senior officer of the United States Army who served in North Africa and Western Europe during World War II, and eventually became General of the Army.
During World War II, his troops referred to Bradly as "The Soldier's General" because of his empathy and benevolence for the soldiers in his command. After the war, Bradley was appointed to head the Veterans Administration, and by the end of his distinguished career he became a five-star General and the first-ever chairman of the Joint Chiefs of Staff.

Born: February 12, 1893, Clark, MO
Died: April 8, 1981, New York City, NY

## Richard Branson

British mega-entrepreneur and billionaire Sir Richard Charles Nicholas Branson began building his vast empire when he launched Virgin Records in 1973. Today Virgin Group holds more than 200 companies in more than 30 countries. He started his first business, a magazine, while aged 16. and then moved into mail-order work. He founded his recored company and record stores, wiich became finacially successful on the back of Mike Oldfirld's best-selling albums. He used the money to invest in many other business ventures, including Virgin Trains and his commercial spaceflight venture Virgin Galactic. His personal wealth is estimated at $5 billion.

Born: July 18, 1950, London, England

## Brasidas of Sparta

Brasidas was a Spartan army officer during the early years of the Peloponnesian War. He is considered by history to have been the most distinguished Spartan officer of that war. He was present at the relief of the siege of Methos, and was badly wounded in action at the famous Battle of Pylas. On recovery he defeated an Athenian force at Megara, commanded troops a the defeat of the Greek Kingdom of Lyncesti, and personally led the charge that routed the superior Athenian force at the siege of Amphipolis. He was mortally wounded in that battle, however, and was buried there; Amphipolis went on to hold yearly games and sacrifices in his honour for many long years afterwards.

Died 422 BCE

## Jean de la Bruyère

Bruyère was an author and philosopher best known for his book 'The Characters, or the Manners of the Age, with The Characters of Theophrastus' which was a scathing examination of class disparities in the 1700s. It was said that his book created many readers and many enemies. Educated at the University of Orléans and called to the bar, he bacame tutor to the royal family of Louis, Prince of Condé. His position gave him access to all of the literary, academic and social figures of the day, most of whom he lampooned in his *Caractères*. He died suddenly of apoplexy shortly after being admitted to the Academy of France.

Born: August 16, 1645, Paris, France
Died: May 11, 1696, Versailles, Yvelines, France

## Bear Bryant

Paul William "Bear" Bryant was an American college football coach who won six national championships at the University of Alabama and retired with what at the time was a record 323 wins, six national championships and thirteen conference championships. Sometimes a controversial figure, he was accused by the Saturday Evening Post of encouraging brutality in his players and fixing matches; he successfully sued for $300,000. A heavy smoker and drinker, Bryant collapsed of a cardiac arrest at age 64 and went into rehab, but continued drinking, had a mild stroke and then died of a heart attack.

Born: September 11, 1913, Cleveland County, Arkansas, AR
Died: January 26, 1983, Tuscaloosa, AL

## John Buchan

John Buchan, 1st Baron Tweedsmuir, was a Scottish novelist and public servant who combined a successful career as an author of thrillers, historical novels, histories and biographies with a parallel career in public life. He wrote propaganda for the British during the First World War. In the 1920s he was an elected Member of Parliament but concentrated on writing successful adventure fiction; his most famous novel from this time is The Thirty-Nine Steps. In 1935 he was raised to the peerage and was appointed Governor-General of Canada, a position he held until his death.

Born: August 26, 1875, Perth, United Kingdom
Died: February 11, 1940, Montreal, Canada

## Arleigh A. Burke

Burke was an admiral of the United States Navy who distinguished himself during World War II and the Korean War, and who served as Chief of Naval Operations during the Eisenhower and Kennedy administrations. From a family of Swedish immigrants originally called Björkgren who lived in Boulder, Colorado, he served for 18 years on battleships and destroyers before the outbreak of World War Two, when he was put in command of two destroyer divisions. He was promoted to Chief of Staff, and after the war to Rear-Admiral and Chief of Naval Operations for the Korean War.

October 19, 1901, Boulder, Colorado
Died: January 1, 1996, Bethesda, Maryland

351

**Edmund Burke**

Edmund Burke was an Irish political philosopher, Whig politician and statesman who is often regarded as the father of modern conservatism. In his work 'A Vindication of Natural Society: or, a View of the Miseries and Evils arising to Mankind from every Species of Artificial Society' he argued in favour of virtue, social manners and the importance of religious institutions. He supported Catholic emancipation and opposed the French Revolution, stating that by destroying the traditional institutions of state and society it destroyed what was good about that society.

Born: January 12, 1729, Dublin, Republic of Ireland
Died: July 9, 1797, Beaconsfield, United Kingdom

**James MacGregor Burns**

Burns was an American Pulitzer Prize-winning presidential biographer, historian, presidential adviser, political scientist, and pioneer on leadership studies. He was the Woodrow Wilson Professor of Government Emeritus at Williams College and Distinguished Leadership Scholar at the James MacGregor Burns Academy of Leadership of the School of Public Policy at the University of Maryland, College Park. His 1978 book "Leadership" remains the required book to read for those involved in business and politics. He coined the term "transformational leadership."

Born: August 3, 1918, Boston, MA
Died: July 15, 2014, Williamstown, MA)

352

## Nolan Bushnell

Founder of Atari Games, Nolan Kay Bushnell was named one of Newsweek's "50 Men Who Changed America." He is considered to be a founding father of the video game industry. He paid his way through college by working at an amusement park, where he became interested in the arcade games. His interests led him to create both Chuck E. Cheese's Pizza-Time Theaters and Atari. He was approached by Steve Jobs to finance his newly-founded Apple Corporation, and offered ownership of a third of the company for $50,000. As he said later, "I was so smart, I said no. It's kind of fun to think about that, when I'm not crying".

Born: February 5, 1943, Clearfield, UT

## Cato the Elder

Cato the Elder, born Marcus Porcius Cato and also known as Cato the Censor, Cato the Wise, and Cato the Ancient, was a Roman senator, soldier, orator, author and historian. At the age of 17 he became a soldier and fought with valor and distinction in The Second Punic War. He was known as a brilliant orator in court and went on to a life in politics. At a time when early Roman strictness, self-discipline, military hardness and rustic simplicity were giving way to Greek permissiveness and modern culture, he tried to preserve Rome's ancestral customs and combat "degenerate" Hellenistic influences.

Born: 234 BCE, Tusculum, Italy
Died: 149 BCE, Roman Republic

## Julius Caesar

Gaius Julius Caesar was a Roman politician, warrior, and general of the late Roman republic. He played a crucial role in the downfall of the Roman Republic and the rise of the Roman Empire. Caesar is regarded by many historians as one of history's greatest military commanders. His victorious conquest of Gaul and his expeditions into Britain and Germany led to his becoming the pre-eminent military power in the Republic. Ordered to stand down, he famously crossed the Rubicon river into Italy with his legion, won the ensuing civil war and became Dictator of Rome.

Born: July 13, 100 BCE, Rome, Italy
Assassinated: March 15, 44 BCE, Rome, Italy

## Andrew Carnegie

Considered the father of modern philanthropy, Andrew Carnegie was a Scottish-American self-made tycoon who led the immense growth of the American steel industry in the late 19th century. He is often identified as one of the richest people and one of the richest Americans ever. He grew up as the son of a handloom weaver. He built a leadership role as a philanthropist for the United States and the British Empire. During the last 18 years of his life, he gave away to charities, foundations, and universities about $350 million, $12.5 billion today, almost 90% of his fortune.

Born: November 25, 1835, Dunfermline, Scotland
Died: August 11, 1919, Lenox, MA

## Herbert Casson

Herbert Newton Casson was a Canadian journalist, publisher, author, and activist who wrote mainly about business and technology. During the course of his career Casson interviewed a Who is Who of history including Presidents Grover Cleveland, Benjamin Harrison, Theodore Roosevelt, Woodrow Wilson, and inventors such as Guglielmo Marconi, Nikola Tesla, Thomas Edison, and Alexander Graham Bell. He wrote 168 books on the subject of business success, founded the business journal *Efficiency*, and gave lectures on factory management.

Born: September 23, 1869, Odessa, Ukraine
Died: September 4, 1951, Surrey, United Kingdom

## Baldassare Castiglione

Castiglione, Count of Casatico was a renowned Italian Renaissance author, courtier, diplomat and soldier. He is mainly remembered for his successful and influential work, 'The Book of the Courtier'. In 1494 at age 15 he began humanist studies in Milan, but on the death of his father five years later inherited the family title and estates, and the attendant political duties. He wrote pastoral plays, songs and sonnets, and was passionately in love with his young wife, but at her untimely death he joined the church, became Ambassdor for the Holy See and Bishop of Avila. He died of the plague shortly afterwards.

Born: December 6, 1478 Casatico, Italy
Died: February 2, 1529, Toledo, Spain

## Catherine the Great

Catherine II of Russia, also known as Catherine the Great, was the most renowned and the longest ruling female leader of Russia, reigning from 1762 until her death in 1796 at the age of 67. Born into an impoverished princely family in Poland, she rose in society thanks to wealthy connections, and was married to the heir to the Empire of Russia, Peter the Third, though she had taken an instant dislike to him when she met him. She overthrew her husband in a coup d'état and went on to expand the Russian Empire by 200,000 square miles.

Born: May 2, 1729, Szczecin, Poland
Died: November 17, 1796, Tsarskoye Selo, Saint Petersburg, Russia

## Bennett Cerf

Bennett Alfred Cerf was an American publisher, and one of the founders of American publishing firm Random House Books. He was an integral part of modernizing the publishing business. While at Random House, Cerf fought the U.S. Customs over their censoring the James Joyce book Ulysses. The Federal judge ruled in favor of Random House and deemed that the book was not obscene. He also published books by Ayn Rand, William Faulkner, James Michener, Truman Capote, Eugene O'Neill, and Theodor Geisel (aka Dr. Seuss).

Born: May 25, 1898, Manhattan, New York City, NY
Died: August 27, 1971, Mount Kisco, NY

## Chanakya, The Indian Machiavelli

Chanakya is one of the most remembered and impressive personalities of ancient India whose contribution to the field of economics, philosophy, and statecraft are studied to this day. He was instrumental in the ascension of Chandra Gupta to become ruler of India. He is traditionally identified as Kau-ilya or Vishnugupt, who authored the two ancient great works, namely Arthashastra (the principles of Economics) and Chanakya Niti (Chanakya's Secrets of Statecraft). Nothing certain is known about his life, and all of the existing accounts are semi-legendary, but it seems probable that he was a Brahmin and minister to the Mauryan emperor Chandra Gupta.

Born: 371 BCE, India
Died: 283 BCE, Pataliputra

## Lord Chesterfield

Philip Dormer Stanhope, 4th Earl of Chesterfield was a British statesman, diplomat and man of letters. An old-fashioned aristocrat, he was educated at Cambridge, went on the Grand Tour of Europe, then took up a position in the House of Lords, and was made Lord of the Bedchamber to the Prince of Wales. He is best remembered for writing 'Letters to His Son on the Art of Becoming a Man of the World and a Gentleman', published in 1774, a series of more than four hundred letters written to his son over a thirty year period instructing him on the ways of the world.

Born: September 22, 1694, London, England
Died: March 24, 1773, London, England

357

## Winston Churchill

Sir Winston Leonard Spencer-Churchill was a British statesman, soldier, author, and artist. He served as the Prime Minister of the United Kingdom from 1940 to 1945 and again from 1951 to 1955. He won the Nobel Prize for Literature in 1953 for his total lifetime body of historical writing. In the First World War, he was blamed for the fiasco of the Battle of Gallipoli, and demoted from his then position as First lord of the Admiralty, but as British Prime Minister during World War Two he is credited for rallying the British people, leading them from defeat to victory.

Born: November 30, 1874, Blenheim Palace, England
Died: January 24, 1965, London, England

## Cicero

Marcus Tullius Cicero was a Roman philosopher, translator, politician, lawyer, orator and political theorist. Born into a wealthy equestrian family, Cicero was instrumental in bringing Greek philosophy to Rome. His writings in Latin have been considered the high-point of classsical prose style, and were influential across Europe not only during the Roman Empire but also from their rediscovery at the start of the Renaissance to the nineteenth century. A fierce opponent of both Julius Caesar and Mark Anthony and a supporter of the old Republican order, he was executed attempting to flee Italy.

Born: January 3, 106 BCE, Arpino, Italy
Assassinated: December 7, 43 BCE, Formia, Italy

## Carl Von Clausewitz

Carl Philipp Gottfried von Clausewitz was a Prussian general and military theorist who stressed the psychological and political aspects of war. Born into a family that made dubious claims of aristocratic inheritance, Clausewitz fought in the Napoleonic Wars, and, after leaving the defeated Prussian army, served with the Russian army at the Battle of Borodino, made famous by its detailed description in Tolstoy's War and Peace. Rejoining the Prussian army as a colonel, Clausewitz's unit was successful in stopping reinforcements arriving to help Napoleon at the Battle of Waterloo.

Born: June 1, 1780, Germany
Died: November 16, 1831, Poland

## Cuthbert Collingwood

Vice Admiral Cuthbert Collingwood, 1st Baron Collingwood, was a British naval commander. His love affair with the sea began at the age of 12 when he joined the Royal Navy. Collingwood was involved in some of the major sea battles of the era. He is best known for taking command of the British fleet during the Battle of Trafalgar, after Admiral Lord Nelson was killed from injuries suffered during the battle. Appointed Commander in Chief of the Mediterranean, his innate decency and his opposition to press-ganging and flogging led to him being called 'father' by the sailors under his command.

Born: September 26, 1748, Newcastle upon Tyne, United Kingdom
Died: March 7, 1810, at sea near Menorca, Spain

## Confucius

Confucius, also known as Kong Qui or K'ung Fu-tzu was a Chinese student of human nature and philosopher. He promoted personal and social morality, justice, family loyalty, respect for elders, veneration of ancestors and respect given to husbands by wives. Born and schooled as a commoner, he became governor of a town and the local minister for crime and law enforcement. After a period of self-imposed exile, he spent his later years exponding his beliefs. He observed that a successful leader had to exercise self-discipline in order to remain modest and treat his followers with empathy.

Born c. 551BCE
Died c. 479 BCE

## Calvin Coolidge

John Calvin Coolidge Jr. became the 30th President of the United States on August 3, 1923, after the sudden death of President Warren G. Harding (1865-1923). An attorney from Vermont, Coolidge worked his way up the hierarchy of Massachusetts state politics, eventually becoming governor of that state. Known as a man who embodied the spirit and hopes of the middle class, he restored public confidence in the White House after scandals involving the previous incumbent. He earned the nickname "Silent Cal" for his calm, resolute and prudent nature.

Born: July 4, 1872, Plymouth Notch, Vermont, VT
Died: January 5, 1933, Northampton, MA

## Charles De Gaulle

Charles André Joseph Marie de Gaulle was a French president, general, warrior, statesman, and writer. During the 1930s he opposed France's reliance on the Maginot Line for defense against Germany. His advice was ignored and by June 1940, German forces easily crushed French troops. De Gaulle refused to recognize the French government's truce with the Germans and escaped to London, where he helped create a French government in exile. He became leader of this resistance known as the Free French. He later went on to become the President of France.

Born: November 22, 1890, Lille, France
Died: November 9, 1970, Colombey-les-Deux-Églises, France

## Max De Pree

Max De Pree was an American businessman and writer. De Pree was the CEO of Herman Miller, Inc. During his time as CEO, Herman Miller grew into a massively profitable Fortune 500 company. From the time he took over as CEO in 1975 until he stepped down in 1986, Herman Miller ranked seventh in terms of total investor returns. He believed in the idea of inclusive corporations, businesses in which all voices are heard, not just the opinions of senior management, fostering 'open communication'. His book 'Leadership is an Art' has sold more than 800,000 copies

Born: October 28, 1924
Died August 8, 2017

## Michael Dell

Michael Saul Dell is an American business magnate, investor, philanthropist, and author. He is the founder and CEO of Dell Technologies, one of the world's leading providers of information technology infrastructure solutions which include Dell, Dell EMC, Pivotal, RSA, SecureWorks, Virtustream and VMware. A born entrepreneur, Dell started making and upgrading computers from kits as a teenager, and set up his first busineess during his first year at college, when he earned more than his teachers. Dropping out of education, he founded his company, then called 'PCs Inc.' with $1,000 in 1984 at the age of 19. His personal fortune is now well over $10 billion.

Born: February 23, 1965, Houston, TX

## W. Edwards Deming

Deming was an American engineer, management guru, author and scientist. He is considered to be the master of continual quality improvement, and the father of management science. He is best known for his work in Japan after World War II, where he trained managers and engineers on the methods for management of quality. His influence was credited with the astounding turnaround of the Japanese economy into a global economic power. He is often referred to as the "father of the third wave of the industrial revolution". President Ronald Reagan awarded him the National Medal of Technology in 1987.

Born: October 14, 1900, Sioux City, IA
Died: December 20, 1993, Washington, D.C.

## Demosthenes

Demosthenes was an Athenian statesman, widely recognized as the one of the greatest ancient Greek orators. He made a living as a professional speech-writer, and began to make political speeches himself when Athens was threatened by the expansion of the power of Phillip II of Macedon. He was one of the leaders in Athens's revolt against Aexander the Great, which was, however, brutally put down. Alexander's commander in the Athenian region sent men to track him down and kill him; he took his own life to escape them. His public speaking was described by his contemporaries as 'like a blazing thunderbolt'.

Born 384 BCE, Athens
Died October 12, 322, Calauria, Argolis

## Diogenes

Diogenes of Sinope was a Greek philosopher and one of the founders of Cynic philosophy. He was known as Diogenes the Cynic. He was a controversial and eccentric figure in his time, making a big show of his poverty and simple life by sleeping in a ceramic jar in the marketplace. He is best known for walking around with a lantern in the daylight, claiming he was searching for an honest man. He publicly criticised Plato, and disrupted his lectures. Captured by pirates, he ended up in Corinth, where his teachings eventually founded the Stoic philosophical tradition.

Born: 412 BCE, Sinop, Turkey
Died: 323 BCE, Corinth, Greece

**Roy E. Disney**

Roy Disney was the nephew of Walt Disney. He spent his entire working career at Disney. Throughout the years, he maintained a steadfast devotion to Walt Disney's founding principles. As chairman of the animation department, he oversaw the making of The Lion King, whose huge success stimulated the Disney company's return to innovative form. It was Roy Disney who ran the collaborations with Pixar that produced Toy Story and Monsters Inc. By the time of his death his fortune was estimated to be $1.2 billion.

Born: January 10, 1930, Los Angeles, CA
Died: December 16, 2009, Newport Beach, CA

**Benjamin Disraeli**

Benjamin Disraeli, 1st Earl of Beaconsfield, was a British statesman and writer who served as Prime Minister of the United Kingdom twice. His early business ventures were a failure and left him in massive debit. After a breakdown he spent the next four years trying to determine what he would do. He decided to enter the political arena. It took four attempts but in 1837 he was elected as Tory candidate. He soon demonstrated that he was a compelling speaker and his career rocketed.

Born: December 21, 1804, Blooms bury, London
Died: April 19, 1881, London, United Kingdom

## Frederick Douglass

Douglass was born into slavery with the name Frederick Augustus Washington Bailey. He was an activist for human rights, including the abolition of slavery, women's rights and Irish home rule. At the age of 20 he escaped from slavery, changed his last name to Douglass (the name of the hero of Sir Walter Scott's The Lady of the Lake) and went on to become one of the most influential African Americans of the nineteenth century. His several biographical books became hugely influential. He summed up his approach as "I would unite with anybody to do right and with nobody to do wrong."

Born: c. February 1818, Talbot County, Maryland
Died: February 20, 1895, Washington, D.C.

## Peter Drucker

Peter Drucker was an Austrian-born American management consultant, educator, and author, whose writings contributed to the philosophical and practical foundations of the modern business corporation. Described as "the founder of modern management", he invented the practice of 'management by objectives and self-control'. He correctly predicted the rise of Japanese economic power, and was the first to recognise and appreciate the emergence of the information society, coining the term 'knowledge worker', people whose line of work requires them to think for a living.

Born: November 19, 1909, Vienna, Austria
Died: November 11, 2005, Claremont, CA

365

## Dwight D. Eisenhower

Dwight David "Ike" Eisenhower was an American politician and general who served as the Supreme Commander of Allied forces in Western Europe during World War II, and as the 34th President of the United States from 1953 until 1961. Raised in Kansas by Pennsylvania Dutch parents, he graduated from West Point in 1915 and joined the army, eventually becoming Brigadier General and Army Chief of Staff. He was the first Supreme Commander of Nato in 1951. His time as President was mostly concerned with the Cold War, limiting Soviet expansion and ending the Korean War.

Born: October 14, 1890, Denison, TX
Died: March 28, 1969, Washington, D.C.

## Queen Elizabeth I

Elizabeth I was the Queen of England and Ireland and brought prosperity and consistency for the 44 years of her reign until her death. She is remembered as a queen who was truly concerned with her people, and used her wit and shrewd mind to avoid political and religious minefields. One of her first actions as queen was the establishment of an English Protestant church. She was the intended victim of several plots and assassination attempts, all of which were foiled by her secret service, and the defeat of the Spanish Armada in 1588 altered geopolitics. She never married, and was celebrated as the Virgin Queen.

Born: September 7, 1533, Greenwich, United Kingdom
Died: March 24, 1603, Richmond, United Kingdom

## Larry Ellison

Lawrence Joseph "Larry" Ellison is an American businessman, entrepreneur, and philanthropist who is co-founder of Oracle Corporation and was CEO from its founding in June of 1977 until September 2014. He currently serves as executive chairman and chief technology officer of Oracle. He went from being a two-time college drop out to multi-billionaire. He credits his unconventional thinking and challenging conventional wisdom as the keys to his success. As of June 2018 he was listed by Forbes magazine as the fifth-wealthiest person in the United States and as the tenth-wealthiest in the world, with a fortune of $54.5 billion.

Born August 17, 1944 Manhattan, New York

### Ralph Waldo Emerson

Emerson, was an American essayist, philosopher, lecturer, and poet who led the transcendentalist movement, which encouraged independent thinking. He gave more than 1,500 public lectures during his life, published dozens of essays, and developed the ideas of individualism and personal freedom. The son of a Unitarian minister, he was ordained in 1829 but resigned in disagreement with the church and with loss of faith. Considered one of the great Romantics, Emerson himself said "I have taught one doctrine, namely, the infinitude of the private man."

Born: May 25, 1803, Boston, MA
Died: April 27, 1882, Concord, MA

### Epictetus

Epictetus was a Stoic philosopher. Born a slave, he went on to eventually gain his freedom and to teach philosophy in Rome for over 25 years. Epictetus taught that philosophy is not a theoretical discipline but a way to live your life every day. Lame from childhood, one account saying that his leg was deliberately broken by his owner, after gaining his freedom he lived a lonely life of extreme simplicity, with few possessions. Despite this, he was admired by the Emperor Hadrian, who became a friend. All of his ideas were written down by his pupil Arrian, who described him as a powerful speaker.

Born 55 AD, Hierapolis, Turkey
Died 135 AD, Nicopolis, Greece

### Ludwig Wilhelm Erhard

Ludwig Wilhelm Erhard was a German statesman and economist who was the chief architect of West Germany's post-World War II economic recovery. He served as the second Chancellor of the Federal Republic of Germany from 1963 to 1966, and the economics minister from 1949 to 1963. He promoted the social market economy that is to this day the underlying principle of German society. In World War II he was sacked by the Nazis from his position in a marketing research company for working towards postwar peace. He became known as a thoughtful, sensitive man who had opposed Nazism.

Born: February 4, 1897, Fürth, Germany
Died: May 5, 1977, Bonn, Germany.

## Harvey S. Firestone

Harvey Samuel Firestone was an American entrepreneur and the founder of the Firestone Tire and Rubber Company, one of the oldest global makers of automobile tires. Before founding his tire company, he worked as a bookkeeper and a salesman. In 1926 he published the book 'Men and Rubber: The Story of Business'. His rubber tires were hugely successful, and he, Henry Ford, and Thomas Edison were considered the three leaders in American industry at the time. All three were part of a very exclusive group titled "The Millionaires' Club", and often worked and vacationed together.

Born: December 20, 1868, Columbiana, OH
Died: February 7, 1938, Miami Beach, FL

## Mary Parker Follett

Mary Follett was an American social worker, management consultant, philosopher and pioneer in the fields of organizational theory and organizational behavior. Follett was one of the first people to apply psychological perception and social science discoveries to the study of organizations. She is considered a pioneer of organizational theory and behavior and coined the term "transformational leadership." She is sometimes referred to as the "Mother of Modern Management". She studied at the University of Cambridge, published many books, and was an advisor to President Theodore Roosevelt.

Born: September 3, 1868, Quincy, MA
Died: December 18, 1933, United Kingdom

## Henry Ford

Ford was the founder of the Ford Motor Company, and the pioneer of the development of the assembly line techniques for mass production. In 1903, he founded the Ford Motor Company, and within five years the company rolled out the first Model T. In order to keep up with the flood of orders for the innovative vehicle, Ford invented revolutionary new mass production procedures, which included the world's first moving assembly line for cars. In 1914, Ford increased the daily pay for an eight hour working day for his employees to $5 which was almost double the $2.34 for a nine hour working day.

Born: July 30, 1863, Greenfield Township, Michigan
Died: April 7, 1947, Fair Lane, Dearborn, MI

## Clarence Francis

Francis was an American business executive and expert on food production and distribution. Later in life, he consulted for the United Nations and President Eisenhower. He originally intended to work for Standard Oil, but by mistake presented himself for employment at the wrong office, and found himself working for a food company. He soon became a leading figure in the industry, and by the time he retired from the General Foods Corporation in 1954 he had become Chairman of the Board of Directors, and was was the American representative on the European Productivity Agency.

Born: December 1, 1888, Staten Island, New York City, NY
Died: 1985

## Viktor E. Frankl

Viktor Emil Frankl was an Austrian neurologist and psychiatrist as well as a Holocaust survivor. Frankl's memoir, 'Man's Search for Meaning', also titled 'Say "Yes" to Life: A Psychologist Experiences the Concentration Camp', has enthralled readers with its depiction of life in Nazi death camps and its lessons for spiritual survival. During World War II, Frankl toiled in four different concentration camps, including Auschwitz, while his parents, brother, and pregnant wife died. Frankl was the founder of logotherapy (from the Greek word logos or "meaning") which is a form of existential analysis.

Born: March 26, 1905, Leopoldstadt, Vienna, Austria
Died: September 2, 1997, Vienna, Austria

## Benjamin Franklin

Franklin is best known as one of the Founding Fathers who created the Declaration of Independence and the Constitution of the United States. Despite having only attended formal schooling until he was 10 years old, Franklin was an acclaimed polymath, leading printer, journalist, author, postmaster, Freemason, politician, inventor, scientist, inventor, diplomat, and statesman. His long list of inventions includes the lightening rod, and bifocal lenses. He founded the University of Pennsylvania and was the first secretary of the American Philosophical Society.

Born: January 17, 1706, Boston, MA
Died: April 17, 1790, Philadelphia, PA

## Frederick the Great

Frederick II was King of Prussia from 1740 until 1786. He was a brilliant military strategist who, in a series of diplomatic ploys and wars against Austria and other powers, immensely enlarged Prussia's territories and made Prussia the leading military power in Europe. He is credited with establishing religious tolerance, and allowed an elementary form of freedom of the press. He reinforced the legal system and instituted the first German code of law. Because of his conquering military success he was idolized by Hitler and other leading Nazis, but a modern re-evaluation has seen him revisioned as an enlightened ruler.

Born January 24, 1712, Berlin, Prussia
Died August 17, 1786, Potsdam, near Berlin, Germany

## Thomas Fuller

Fuller was an English churchman, historian and author who had the keen ability to write with deep insight into human psychology. He is remembered for being both prolific and clever. As a young curate he attracted attention for his oratory. During the Civil War he joined the Royalist side and preached sermons in their favour while with the king at Oxford. He continued to write, publish and preach during Oliver Cromwell's commonwealth, and after the restoration he was admitted Doctor of Divinity at Cambridge. His most famous work, Worthies of England, was published posthumously.

Born June 19, 1608, Northamptonshire, England
Died Aug. 16, 1661, London, England

## John Kenneth Galbraith

John 'Ken' Galbraith was a Canadian economist, public official, and diplomat, and a leading proponent of 20th-century American liberalism. He wrote 48 books, including novels and collections of essays. His 'American capitalism' trilogy, 'The Affluent Society' (1958), 'The New Industrial State' (1967), and 'Economics and the Public Purpose' (1973) were hailed as a major contribution to the theory of economics. He argued that the market power of large corporations allowed them to set prices, removing the power of the customer, while for him the empowered individual was most important.

Born: October 15, 1908, Ontario Canada
Died April 29, 2006 Cambridge, MA

## Mahatma Gandhi

Mohandas Karamchand Gandhi was a lawyer, politician, social activist and writer who is best known for being the leader of the Indian independence movement in British-ruled India. His doctrine of nonviolent protest to achieve political change and social progress is credited with bringing the overthrow of British rule. He trained as a lawyer in London before working for the rights of expatriate Indians in South Africa. Returning home he became leader of the Indian National Congress in 1921. He called his movement 'satyagraha', which means "appeal to, or reliance on the Truth".

Born: October 2, 1869, Porbandar, India
Assassinated: January 30, 1948, New Delhi, India

## John W. Gardner

John William Gardner had a varied and productive career as an educator, public official, and political reformer. Perhaps best known as the founder of the lobby Common Cause, he was the author of several best-selling books on the themes of leadership, achieving personal and societal excellence. He championed campaign finance reform and introduced Medicare as Secretary of Health, Education and Welfare in the heyday of President Lyndon B. Johnson's Great Society. He served as a Marine during World War II and in the O.S.S., the precursor to the C.I.A.

Born: October 8, 1912, Los Angeles, CA
Died: February 16, 2002, Palo Alto, CA

## Bill Gates

William Henry "Bill" Gates III is best known as the co-founder of Microsoft. He is an entrepreneur, philanthropist and author. He left Harvard University in 1975 to fully devote himself to Microsoft. At the time most people in the computer industry believed in sharing the creation and writing of code. Gates insisted that computer code should always be paid for. His anti-competitive business practises were the subject of many court battles, including the anti-trust case 'United States vs Microsoft'. From 1995 to 2017, he held the title of the richest person in the world in all but four of those years, though now he has been overtaken by Amazon's Jeff Bezos.

Born: October 28, 1955 Seattle, WA

## Harold S. Geneen

Harold Sydney Geneen was an American businessman who forged ITT Corp. into the model for the global conglomerate during his 18 year rule as its CEO. Trained as an accountant, he went on to revolutionize how corporations functioned. When he was named president and CEO of ITT in 1959, it had less than $800,000 a year in revenue. When he retired as CEO in 1977, ITT was the 11th largest industrial company in the U.S., with more than 375,000 employees and $16.7 billion in revenue. During this period ITT funded the overthrow of President Allende in Chile, with help from the CIA.

Born: January 22, 1910, Bournemouth, Dorset, England
Died November 21, 1997, New York City

## Louis V. Gerstner, Jr.

Louis Gerstner is an American businessman, best known for his time as chairman of the board and CEO of IBM from April 1993 until 2002 when he retired. Initially successful at American Express as president in charge of AmEx cards and travellers cheques, Gerstner increased its membership by almost four times. Outcompeted and undercut by Microsoft, a now-struggling IBM hired Gerstner to turn around its fortunes. He laid off 100,000 workers, made the company more competitive, and personally amassed a fortune of hundreds of millions while raising IBM's market capitalization from $29 billion to $168 billion.

Born: March 1, 1942, Mineola, NY

## Arnold Glasow

Arnold Henry Glasow was an American businessman who started his own business after the Great Depression and went on to achieve great success. His business was a humor magazine that he marketed to firms nationally, which firms would turn it into their "house organ" to send to their customers. He carried on this business for over 60 years, publishing his first book at age 92. The book is titled, "Glasow's Gloombusters," one of the many titles he put on his work during his career. He was cited frequently in the Wall Street Journal, Forbes, the Chicago Tribune and many other major organs.

Born 1095, Fond-du-lac, Wisconsin
Died 1998, Freeport, Illinois

## Johann Wolfgang Von Goethe

Goethe was a German statesman, poet, playwright, novelist, and natural philosopher and is best known for his two-part poetic drama Faust (1808-1832), which he started around the age of twenty three and didn't finish till shortly before his death sixty years later. The author of novels, epic and lyric poetry, prose and verse dramas, memoirs, an autobiography, literary and aesthetic criticism, and treatises on botany, anatomy, and colour, he is considered one of the greatest contributors of the German Romantic period. He was also active throughout his life as an administrator of public works.

Born: August 28, 1749, Free City of Frankfurt
Died: March 22, 1832, Weimar, Germany

## Roberto Goizueta

Roberto Críspulo Goizueta Cantera was Chairman, Director, and CEO of The Coca-Cola Company from August 1980 until his death in October 1997. Goizueta was born in Cuba, and took a minor job in Coca-Cola in response to a *Help Wanted* ad in the local paper. When Fidel Castro took power in a communist revolution Goizueta was in Florida with his family; they defected and he worked for Coca-Cola in the USA, slowly rising up the hierarchy until becoming its president in 1979, a post he held for 16 years until his death from smoking-related cancer.

Born: November 18, 1931, Havana, Cuba
Died: October 18, 1997, Atlanta, GA

## Jim Goodnight

Goodnight is the co-founder and CEO of SAS, the world's leading business analytics software vendor. Goodnight has led the company since its founding in 1976, overseeing continuous years of revenue growth and profitability. While working as a software programmer for a company that was building electronic equipment for NASA's Apollo program, Goodnight experienced a toxic work culture that resulted in an annual turnover rate of over 50 percent. This experience forged his views on organizational culture and his future role as a leader. His devotion to ensuring a healthy work-life balance has made SAS No. 1 on the Great Place to Work Institute's multinational ranking.

Born: January 6, 1943, Salisbury, NC

## Baltasar Gracián

Baltasar Gracián y Morales, SJ was a Spanish Jesuit philosopher and writer. His writings were extoled by Nietzsche and Schopenhauer. Studying theology and becoming ordained, Gracián repeatedly disobeyed his superiors and was exiled. He wrote and published his most famous work, the Criticón, without permission. A long allegorical and philosophical novel published in three volumes, it was widely celebrated in Europe at the time. He also published a book of three hundred maxims, called 'Oráculo Manual y Arte de Prudencia', The Oracle Manual and Art of Discretion.

Born: January 8, 1601, Belmonte de Gracián, Spain
Died: December 6, 1658, Tarazona, Spain

## Ulysses S. Grant

Ulysses S. Grant was the 18th President of the United States. During the later years of America's Civil War he became the Commanding General of the United States Army, ultimately leading it to victory. He reluctantly accepted the role of President, saying "I have been forced into it in spite of myself. I could not back down without, as it seems to me, leaving the contest for power for the next four years between mere trading politicians, the elevation of whom, no matter which party won, would lose to us, largely, the results of the costly war which we have gone through."

Born: April 27, 1822, Point Pleasant, OH
Died: July 23, 1885, Wilton, NY

## Heinz Wilhem Guderian

Guderian was a German general and fast-moving mechanized warfare expert. He is credited with recognizing the potential of the military tactic called blitzkrieg (German for "lightning war") and using it to help bring about decisive victories in Poland, France, and the Soviet Union early in World War II. After the German defeat at Stalingrad, Hitler appointed him Inspector General of Armoured Troops, reporting directly to the Fuhrer on the rebuilding and training of the German Panzer divisions. After the war he was not charged with any war crime and went on to advise the West German Bundeswehr.

Born June 17, 1888, Kulm, Germany [now Chełmno, Poland
Died May 14, 1954, Schwangau bei Füssen, West Germany

## David Hackworth

Colonel David Haskell Hackworth, known as "Hack," was a highly decorated, extremely unconventional former career American Army office who became a combat legend in Vietnam. He also fought in World War II, and the Korean War. He was awarded nine Silver Stars, four Legions of Merit, eight Bronze Stars, eight Purple Hearts and four Army Commendation Medals, among numerous others. His brilliant career came to an end when he publicly and viciously excoriated his superiors over the Vietnam War. His investigation into Admiral Mike Boorda's improper wearing of medals led to the Admiral's suicide.

Born: November 11, 1930, California
Died: May 4, 2005, Tijuana, Mexico

## Hadrian

Caesar Traianus Hadrianus Augustus was Roman Emperor from 117 AD to 138 AD. He is known for his wise and just rule. Though his rule was a time filled mostly with peace, he spent twelve of his twenty one year reign outside of Rome inspecting the provinces, seeing how things were being done and what could be done better. His keen sense of curiosity and sharp intellect made him a great administrator. An admirer of Greek culture, Hadrian made or completed several Greek-inspired monuments in Rome and made Athens the cultural capital of the empire.

Born: January 24, 76 AD
Died: July 10, 138 AD, Baiae, Italy

## William F. Halsey

William Frederick Halsey Jr., known as Bill Halsey or "Bull", was an American Navy admiral whose aggressive fighting style led to many naval victories during World War II. He was a fierce proponent of using aircraft carriers for warfare and never shied away from a battle. Appointed Commander, South Pacific Area he led the Allied forces at the Battle of Guadalcanal and the Battle for Leyte Gulf, a contender for the largest naval battle in history. He announced the Japanese surrender to those serving under him as: "Cessation of hostilities. War is over. If any Japanese airplanes appear, shoot them down in a friendly way."

Born: October 30, 1882, Elizabeth, NJ
Died: August 16, 1959, Fishers Island, New York, NY

## Dag Hammarskjold

Dag Hjalmar Agne Carl Hammarskjöld was a Swedish economist, diplomat, and author, who served as the second Secretary General of the United Nations for eight years until his death in a plane crash. Hammarskjöld posthumously received the Nobel Peace Prize in 1961, having been nominated before his death. John F. Kennedy called him, "the greatest statesman of our century." He has been credited with having coined the term "planned economy." He spent much of his tenure trying to secure the peaceful decolonisation of Africa, which may have led to his plane being shot down over the Congo.

Born: July 29, 1905, Jönköping, Sweden
Died: September 18, 1961, Ndola, Zambia

## Hannibal

Hannibal Barca was a Carthaginian general, considered one of the greatest military leaders of recorded history. He commanded the Carthaginian forces against Rome in the Second Punic War (218–201 BCE) and almost defeated the Roman Empire. He famously marched an army from Spain that included hundreds of war elephants over the Alps into Italy. He occupied Italy for 15 years without quite conquering and destroying Rome, which was eventually able to counter-attack, destroy Carthage and win the war. He continued to oppose Rome in exile until his death.

Born 247 BCE, Carthage
Died in either 183, or 182 BCE

## B.H. Liddell Hart

Captain Sir Basil H. Liddell Hart was a renowned English warfare strategist, author, soldier and military theorist. His theories on strategy were conceived during his time as a soldier in the ferocious trench warfare of World War I. He was exposed to gas warfare which led to his early retirement from the army, and lifelong health issues. Between the wars he wrote a serie of books on military history and tactics, looking to learn from the disastrous loss of life in WWI. After the Second World War, Captain Hart was influential in the rehabilitation of West Germany and the establishing of the Bundeswehr.

Born: October 31, 1895, Paris, France
Died: January 29, 1970, Marlow, United Kingdom

## William Hazlitt

Hazlitt was an English writer, drama and literary critic, painter, social commentator, and philosopher best known for his humanistic essays. He is now thought of as one of the greatest critics and essayists in the history of the English language. He was fired from an early age by the ideals of liberty and human rights, and held a lifelong interest in human psychology and motivation. His essays covered a very broad spectrum from prizefighters to sonnets, but were always beautifully written, and full of general reflections about human nature, society and the nature of human folly.

Born: April 10, 1778 Maidstone, United Kingdom
Died: September 18 1830, Soho, London, United Kingdom

382

Patrick Henry

Henry was an American attorney, planter and politician and American Revolution-era orator who became known for his uncommon ability to simplify his political ideology into the language of the common man. He is most famous for his quote "Give me liberty or give me death." Henry was a prominent leader in the revolutionary opposition to the British monarchy, but only accepted the new federal government after the passage of the Bill of Rights, for which he was a key figure in its creation. Self-trained as a lawyer, Henry was well known for his oratory during his lifetime.

Born: May 29, 1736, Studley, Virginia
Died: June 6, 1799, Brookneal, VA

Heraclitus

Heraclitus of Ephesus was a Greek philosopher. He is best known for his doctrines that the Universe and therefore all of life are constantly changing, and that opposites are the nature of existence and beneficial. Heraclitus was born into an affluent family, but he rejected his fortune and went to live in the mountains. He argued that only change is constant, that 'no man steps into the same river twice', and that all things come into being through strife, but criticised humanity for wrongdoing and lack of wisdom, becoming known as a loner and a misanthrope.

Born: 535 BCE, Ephesus, Turkey
Died: 475 BCE, Ephesus, Turkey

## Herodotus

Herodotus of Halicarnassus has been known since antiquity as 'The Father of History'. He was the first person ever to write on historical subjects using systematic investigation, checking source materials, using first hand accounts, and looking always to tell the true story rather than one that glorified or vilified its subject or presented legendary material as truth, thereby successfully liberating history from myth. His very truthfulness and simple desire to tell the real story led to hostility in his own lifetime, but modern historians consider him a reliable source.

Born c. 484 BC Halicarnassus, Turkey
Died c. 425 BC Thurii, Calabria or Pella, Macedon

## Dee Hock

Hock is a former local bank executive who went on to found the Visa credit card network. He was working as an ordinary bank official when his employer was franchised by the Bank of America to create a credit card system. By a series of chance developments he ended up managing what was to become VISA. After it became a huge success, Hock gave up the corporate life in 1984 and spent ten years in relative isolation running a small farm. In explanation he said "Through the years, I have greatly feared and sought to keep at bay the four beasts that inevitably devour their keeper – Ego, Envy, Avarice, and Ambition."

Born: March 21, 1929

## Eric Hoffer

Hoffer was an American social philosopher with a keen insight into human nature. He is considered to be one of the most brilliant thinkers of the 20th century. The author of ten books, he was awarded the Presidential Medal of Freedom in February 1983. His book The True Believer: Thoughts on the Nature of Mass Movements, explained how and why mass movements develop. Born in the Bronx to German immigrants, Hoffer lost then regained his sight, lost his parents, became an itinerant worker and gold prospector, but through constant reading started to write seriously about humanity.

Born: July 25, 1898, The Bronx, New York City, NY
Died: May 21, 1983, San Francisco, CA

### Grace Hopper

Grace Brewster Murray Hopper was a U.S. Navy Rear Admiral, computer software pioneer and computer scientist. She earned a PhD in mathematics before joining the navy, and started developing the first modern computers during World War II, creating the first English-language compiler. Her early work on the important computer language COBOL earned her the later nickname 'Grandma COBOL'. She was a pioneer of replacing large centralised systems with distributed ones. She was awarded the National Medal of Technology and the Presidential Medal of Freedom.

Born: December 9, 1906, New York City, NY
Died: January 1, 1992, Arlington County

## Horace

Quintus Horatius Flaccus was a Roman soldier and lyric poet. He wrote satires, odes, maxims and autobiographical verse. It was said of his writings that "he can be lofty sometimes, yet he is also full of charm and grace, versatile in his figures, and felicitously daring in his choice of words." The son of a freed slave who managed to rise in society, Horace was educated in Athens, at the Academy. He was immediately caught up in the power struggle between Mark Anthony and Augustus at the beginning of the Roman Empire; fighting for the wrong side he was given an amnesty and spent the rest of his life at the imperial court.

Born December 65 BCE, Venusia, Italy
Died Nov. 27, 8 BCE, Rome, Italy

## Paul R. Howe

Special Forces/Delta Operator MSG Paul R. Howe is a retired US Army Delta Force operator. He served in the Army for over 20 years, and is a veteran of the Battle of Mogadishu, popularized in the movie Black Hawk Down. Since retiring from the Army, Howe has remained active in the professional tactical community, operating a training company, Combat Shooting and Tactics, and consulting for law enforcement and military training across the United States. He is was awarded the Bronze Star with V Device for Valor. His influential book is "Leadership and Training for the Fight: Using Special Operations Principles to Succeed in Law Enforcement, Business, and War".

# Tony Hsieh

Hsieh is an internet entrepreneur and venture capitalist, and CEO of Internet shoe and clothing web site Zappos. He graduated with a computer science degree from Harvard, where he used to sell pizzas on campus. After college and a brief (5 months) disappointing stint in the corporate world, he went on to co-found LinkExchange, which he ended up selling to Microsoft for $265 million. He received the Ernst & Young Entrepreneur Of The Year award for the Northern California region in 2007. He founded the venture capital firm Venture Frogs after he was dared to do so. He is a major redevelopment investor in Downtown Las Vegas, where he lives.

Born: December 12, 1973, Illinois

# Thomas Huxley

Thomas Henry Huxley was an English biologist, known as "Darwin's Bulldog" for his championing of Charles Darwin's theory of evolution. Huxley was one of the first advocates of Darwin's theory of evolution by natural selection, and was a dominant force in the advancement of its acceptance among both scientists and the public. Despite being born into a family with financial difficulties, Huxley taught himself Latin, Greek, German, Logic and Geology and became an expert on both vertibrates and invertibrates, before being awarded the Gold Prize in anatomy and physiology at London.

Born: May 4, 1825, Ealing, London, United Kingdom
Died: June 29, 1895, Eastbourne, United Kingdom

## Lee Iacocca

Legendary CEO Lido Anthony "Lee" Iacocca is an American automobile executive best known for leading the development of Ford Mustang while at the Ford Motor Company in the 1960's. and then he became famous for navigating the Chrysler Corporation away from bankruptcy toward record profits in the 1980's. He was named the 18th-greatest American CEO of all time by Portfolio magazine. Born to Italian immigrants who ran a hot dog restaurant in Pennsylvania's steel belt, he began his career in engineering, but made his breakthrough as assistant sales manager for Ford with an innovative campaign that went national.

Born: October 15, 1924, Allentown, PA

## Tokugawa Ieyasu

Tokugawa Ieyasu, original name Matsudaira Takechiyo, also called Matsudaira Motoyasu, was the founder of the last shogunate in Japan. He was known as a brilliant general and gifted leader. Born into a samurai family at a turbulent time in Japanese history, he was abducted at age five; his abductor threatened to kill him if his father did not renounce his loyalties, but his father said that sacrificing his son would instead be a proof of those loyalties. He wasn't killed, and went on to fight a lifetime of battles and political intrigues before being declared Shogun by the emperor when he was aged 60.

Born Jan. 31, 1543, Okazaki, Japan
Died June 1, 1616, Sumpu

## Isocrates

Isocrates was an ancient Greek orator, rhetorician, and teacher to many of the eminent men of Greece. later antiquity considered him one of the great 'Attic orators' the ten most celebrated speakers and logographers of the ancient world. Born into a wealthy family in Athens, he was in his youth a friend of Socrates. He started his career as a paid speech writer, and soon set up his own school for rhetoric. He was so successful that he was able to command high prices for his speeches and make his school very select and elite, as a consequence of this he amassed a fortune.

Born: 436 BCE, Athens, Greece
Died: 338 BCE, Athens, Greece

## Reggie Jackson

Reginald Martinez "Reggie" Jackson, nicknamed "Mr. October" for his five appearances in the World Series, is an American former professional baseball right fielder who played 21 seasons for the Kansas City / Oakland Athletics, Baltimore Orioles, New York Yankees, and California Angels. At high school Jackson fractured five cervical vertebrae playing football, which caused him to spend six weeks in the hospital and another month in a neck cast. Doctors told him that he might never walk again, let alone play. Defying the odds, he hit 563 career home runs and was an American League All-Star for 14 seasons. He was inducted into the Baseball Hall of Fame in 1993.

Born: May 18, 1946, Wyncote, PA

## Stonewall Jackson

Thomas Jonathan "Stonewall" Jackson
was a U.S. Army officer who fought with
distinction during the Mexican American
War and was a Confederate general during
the American Civil War. After graduating
from the U.S. Academy at West Point,
Jackson enlisted in the Mexican-American
War. He went on to become a general for the Confederate Army
during America's Civil War. He earned a reputation as a brilliant
leader and was considered a military legend. Jackson was accidently
shot by his own troops which led to an arm being amputated. He died
from pneumonia eight days later.

Born: January 21, 1824, Clarksburg, WV
Died: May 10, 1863, Guinea, Virginia, VA

## William James

James was an American philosopher and
psychologist, a leader of the philosophical
movement of Pragmatism and of the
psychological movement of functionalism.
He is often called the "Father of American
psychology." Born into a wealthy family,
he trained as a physician and taught
anatomy at Harvard, but never practiced medicine. Instead he
pursued his interests in psychology and philosophy, writing works
in epistemology, education, metaphysics, psychology, religion, and
mysticism. He was often seriously ill, leading to depression and
suicidal thoughts, but managed to write through the pain.

Born: January 11, 1842, New York City, NY
Died: August 26, 1910, Chocorua, NH

## Thomas Jefferson

Jefferson was an American Founding Father, principle author of the Declaration of Independence and the Statute of Virginia for Religious Freedom, third president of the United States (1801–1809), and founder of the University of Virginia (1819). He served as a public official, historian, lawyer, philosopher, and plantation owner, and was also a surveyor, mathematician and architect. He personally organized the Louisiana Purchase, doubling territory of the United States, and signed signed the Act Prohibiting Importation of Slaves. He was an advocate of religious freedom and tolerance.

Born: April 13, 1743, Shadwell, VA
Died: July 4, 1826, Monticello, VA

## Jiang Taigong

Jiang Taigong, also known as Lu Shang and Jiang Ziya, was the prime minister for the first Zhou emperor and his loyalty and vision in governing spread his fame throughout China. As the most notable Prime Minister employed by King Wen and King Wu, he was declared "the master of strategy". He was credited with the feat of writing the first military strategic book Liutao (Six Secret Strategic Teachings), considered one of the Seven Military Classics of Ancient China. After his death he was often credited with supernatural powers. In the Tang Dynasty he was accorded his own state temple as the martial patron and thereby attained officially sanctioned status approaching that of Confucius.

He lived in 11th century BCE.

**Steve Jobs**

Jobs was an adopted child who was intelligent but aimless. He explored different ventures before starting Apple Computer with Steve Wozniak in 1976. Apple's cutting edge products (iPod, iPhone, iTunes, and the iPad), led the evolution of modern technology. The breakthrough Apple Mackintosh in 1984 created the dektop publishing industry. Jobs was pushed out of Apple in 1985 and returned more than a decade later, when he also became chairman and majority shareholder of Pixar. He died in 2011, following a long battle with pancreatic cancer.

Born: February 24, 1955, San Francisco, CA
Died: October 5, 2011, Palo Alto, CA

**Lyndon Johnson**

Lyndon Baines Johnson became the 36th president of the United States following the November 1963 assassination of President John F. Kennedy. During his administration, Johnson launched the "Great Society" social service programs with the aim of eliminating racial injustice and poverty. He signed the Civil Rights Act into law, and bore the pressure and stress of intense national hostility to his massive expansion of American involvement in the Vietnam War. He balked at running for a second full term in office and retired to his ranch in Texas.

Born: August 27, 1908, Stonewall, TX
Died: January 22, 1973, Stonewall, TX

# John Paul Jones

Admiral John Paul Jones was the United States' most well-known naval commander of the American Revolutionary War. He is sometimes referred to as one of the "Fathers of the American Navy". Originally a Scottish commander in the British navy, he was forced to flee after killing a fellow crewmember with a sword. Arriving in the Colony of Virginia he soon commanded American ships against the British. His time was however controversial, with his enemies calling him a pirate, and after the Revolutionary War he moved to Imperial Russia, where he rose to the rank of Rear Admiral.

Born: July 6, 1747, Kirkcudbright, Scotland
Died: July 18, 1792, Paris, France

# Michael Jordan

Michael Jeffrey Jordan is an American retired professional basketball player, and businessman. Jordan tried out for his high school basketball team during his sophomore year and failed to make the team. He went on to lead the Chicago Bulls to six NBA championships and won the Most Valuable Player Award five times. He also won six NBA Finals Most Valuable Player (MVP) Awards, nine All-Defensive First Team honors, fourteen NBA All-Star Game selections, three All-Star Game MVP Awards, three steals titles, and the 1988 NBA Defensive Player of the Year Award. He is sometimes referred to as 'the greatest basketball player of all time'.

Born: February 17, 1963, Brooklyn, New York City, NY

## Julian the Apostate

Flavius Claudius Julianus, known as 'Julian the Apostate', was Roman Emperor from 361 to 363, as well as a notable philosopher and author in Greek. Raised in the imperial court by a Gothic slave who gave him an excellent education, Julius was appointed Caesar of the eastern Empire and went on to command legions in crushing victories. Becoming overall emperor, he restored the old customs and religion, and embarked on a major campaign against Rome's greatest rival the Persian Sassanid empire, but was murdered near the Upper Tigris, presumably by his Christian enemies.

Born AD 332
Died AD 363

## A.P.J. Abdul Kalam

Avul Pakir Jainulabdeen Abdul Kalam, better known as A.P.J. Abdul Kalam, was the 11th President of India from 2002 to 2007. He spent four decades working as a scientist and science administrator, and was instrumental in developing India's civilian space program and military missile development. He was sometimes referred to as the "Missile Man," and the "People's President." After serving a single term, he reurned to a life of writing, education, public service and public speaking. He launched a programme for the youth of India called the 'What Can I Give Movement', with a central theme of defeating corruption.

Born: October 15, 1931, Rameswaram, India
Died: July 27, 2015, Shillong, India

## Ingvar Kamprad

Ingvar Feodor Kamprad was a Swedish business mogul. He was the founder of IKEA, a Swedish retail company specializing in furniture. He began his commercial interestes selling matches at the age of 5. He founded IKEA in 1943 at the age of 17, selling replicas of is uncle's kitchen table. In 1956, Kamprad pioneered the concept of letting buyers purchase their furniture in pieces and assemble it themselves. His idea would eventually be called flatpacking, and cut costs for IKEA while saving the consumer money. In March 2010, Forbes magazine estimated Kamprad's fortune at US$23 billion.

Born: March 30, 1926, Agunnaryd, Sweden
Died: January 27, 2018, Smaland, Sweden

## Herb Kelleher

Herbert "Herb" David Kelleher is the co-founder, Chairman Emeritus and former CEO of Southwest Airlines, which is one of the first airlines to offer low-cost fares by eliminating extra services and using secondary airports to offer very low fares. Southwest Airlines has had over 43 consecutive years of yearly profitability, a record unsurpassed in the U.S. airline industry. He was responsible for creating a corporate culture that was fun to work in, and was called 'perhaps the best CEO in America'. Kelleher was inducted into the Junior Achievement U.S. Business Hall of Fame in 2004, and won the Bower Award for Business Leadership in 2003.

Born: March 12, 1931, Camden, NJ

## John F. Kennedy

John Fitzgerald "Jack" Kennedy, commonly referred to by his initials JFK, was an American politician who served as the 35th President of the United States from January 1961 until his assassination in November 1963. He served in World War II as a Navy officer. He was awarded the Navy and Marine Corps Medal for heroism and the Purple Heart Medal for injuries. His tenure as president was marked by the high point of East-West tension in the Cold War; he launched the Bay of Pigs invasion of Cuba and, later, nearly presided over the start of thermonuclear war during the Cuban Missile Crisis.

Born: May 29, 1917, Brookline, MA
Died: November 22, 1963, Dallas, TX

## Robert F. Kennedy

Robert Francis "Bobby" Kennedy, sometimes referred to by his initials RFK, was an American politician. He was the brother of President John F. Kennedy. He served as the U.S. attorney general from 1961 to 1964 and as a U.S. senator from New York from 1965 to 1968 until his assassination. As attorney general he fought organized crime and pushed for civil rights for African Americans. He was against the Vietnam War and a tireless champion for the poor and minorities. He was an advocate for issues related to human rights and social justice and formed a relationship with Martin Luther King Jr.

Born: November 20, 1925, Brookline, MA
Assassinated: June 6, 1968, Los Angeles, CA

# Genghis Khan

Genghis Khan (Genghis="Universal" and Khan="leader" or "ruler", born Temüjin ("of iron" or "blacksmith"), was the founder of the Mongol Empire, which he created by banding the nomadic tribes together. By the time of his death, he had conquered a total land mass that was the size of the continent of Africa. He is remembered for being shrewd, brutal, and ferocious, and has been accused of genocide. He granted religious freedom, eliminated torture, encouraged trade and even created the first international postal system. Under the Mongol Empire the Silk Road trade route hade its zenith.

Born: 1162, Delüün Boldog
Died: August 18, 1227, Western Xia

# Martin Luther King Jr.

Martin Luther King Jr. was a Baptist minister and social activist, who led the Civil Rights Movement in the United States from the mid-1950s until his assassination in 1968. Born into a religious family in Atlanta Georgia, King was regularly whipped by his father until he was 15. Ordained in the ministry, King formed the Southern Christian Leadership Conference with other activists to harness the moral authority and organizing power of black churches to conduct nonviolent protests in the service of civil rights reform. He was one of the organisers of the celebrated March on Washington.

Born: January 15, 1929, Atlanta, GA
Died: April 4, 1968, Memphis, TN

**Alfred Korzybski**

Alfred Habdank Skarbek Korzybski was a Polish American scholar, engineer, military officer, and exceptional observer of human behavior. He developed a field called general semantics, which he considered as both different, and more complete than, the field of semantics. He argued that our knowledge of the world is limited by our senses and the inadequate languages we have developed since words are merely noises that must be interpreted by whomever we're speaking to. Words are mere symbols and not reality. He promoted becoming inwardly quiet, calling it "silence on the objective levels".

Born: July 3, 1879, Warsaw, Poland
Died: March 1, 1950, Lakeville, Salisbury, CT

**Ray Kroc**

Raymond Albert Kroc was an American businessman best known for turning McDonald's into the most successful fast food company in the world. At the age of 15, Kroc lied about his age so he could serve as a Red Cross ambulance driver during World War I. After the war, he spent the next two decades working as a paper cup salesman, milkshake machine salesman, pianist, and DJ. In the 1950's he met the McDonalds brothers and began working with them. By 1961 he had purchased the company. Kroc was included in Time 100: The Most Important People of the Century.

Born: October 5, 1902, Oak Park, IL
Died: January 14, 1984, San Diego, CA

## John P. Kotter

Dr. John Paul Kotter is regarded as one of the premiere thought leaders on the topics of leadership and change. A Professor of Leadership, Emeritus, at the Harvard Business School, Kotter was educated at MIT, where he was awarded a Bachelor of Science in electrical engineering and a Master of Science in Management. Kotter then completed his Doctor of Business Administration at Harvard Business School. He is the author of 20 books, 12 of which have been business bestsellers and two of which are overall New York Times bestsellers. His international bestseller 'Leading Change' (1996), is considered to be the seminal work in the field of change management.

Born: February 25, 1947, San Diego, CA

## Tom Landry

Thomas Wade "Tom" Landry was an American football player and coach. He is ranked as one of the best coaches in National Football League history and single handedly recreated the game with creative formations, and tactics. He was the first coach in the NFL to use computers to help gain an edge in every aspect of the game. In addition to his record 20 consecutive winning seasons from 1966 to 1985, during his 29 seasons as the head coach of the Dallas Cowboys, he led the team to win the Super Bowl five times, resulting in the Cowboys receiving the label of "America's Team".

Born: September 11, 1924, Mission, TX
Died: February 12, 2000, Dallas, TX

## Jean de La Fontaine

Jean de La Fontaine was a French classical author and one of the most widely read French poets and prose writers of the 17th century. He is particularly well-known for his twelve books of fables, developed from Aesop and told in free verse and prose, and he also wrote tales and dramatic works. He became part of the quartet of the Rue du Vieux Colombier, consisting of La Fontaine, Racine, Boileau and Molière. He was not without his critics, the second edition of his Tales received police condemnation, and his accession to the Academy was opposed for many years, but he was eventually accepted.

Born: July 8, 1621, Château-Thierry, France
Died: April 13, 1695, Neuilly-sur-Seine, France

## Francois Duc de La Rochefoucauld

François VI, duc de La Rochefoucauld, also called (until 1650) Prince de Marcillac, was a French classical author who had been one of the most active rebels of the series of civil wars in France between 1648 and 1653 during the reign of the widely despised Louis XIV. He eventually became the leading exponent of the maxim, a French literary form of short clever sayings that expresses a harsh or paradoxical truth with brevity. He is also well-known for his successful memoirs, which were, however, largely plagiarised. His 504 maxims were his own, however,. and were much admired in the 19th Century.

Born: September 15, 1613, Paris, France
Died: March 17, 1680, Paris, France

## Tommy Lasorda

Thomas Charles "Tommy" Lasorda is a former American Major League Baseball player and manager who spent over 60 years in the Los Angeles Dodgers organization. He was inducted into the National Baseball Hall of Fame in 1997. His many awards include porting News Minor League Manager of the Year, UPI & AP Manager of the Year, AP Manager of the Year, Baseball America Manager of the Year, Sporting News Co-Manager of the Year, and the Amos Alonzo Stagg Coaching Award presented by the United States Sports Academy. Now in his nineties, he continues to representing the Dodgers at speaking engagements.

Born: September 22, 1927, Norristown, PA

## T.E. Lawrence

Thomas Edward Lawrence, commonly known as Lawrence of Arabia, was a British soldier, author, archaeologist, and diplomat. He is renowned for his part in the Great Arab Revolt which he later wrote about in his memoir The Seven Pillars of Wisdom. He began his career working as an archaeologist in Syria for the British Museum, where he learned Arabic. Stationed in Egypt from the outbreak of hostilities, Lawrence became Liason Officer during the Sinai and Palestine Campaign, and eventually led the capture of Damascus. After the war he worked for the Foreign Office.

Born: 16 August 16, 1888, Tremadog, Carnarvonshire, Wales
Died: May 19, 1935 Bovington Camp, Dorset, England

## John A. Lejeune

John Archer Lejeune was a United States Marine Corps major general, the 13th Commandant of the Marine Corps, and the key person to transform the Marines from a 19th century naval infantry into an efficient amphibious fighting force during World War II. He was affectionately  referred to as the "Greatest of all Leathernecks" and, "The Marine's Marine." Marine Corps Base Camp Lejeune in North Carolina is named in his honor. He served for 40 years in the Marine Corps including commanding the U.S. Army's 2nd Division during World War I.

Born : January 10, 1867, Pointe Coupee Parish, Louisiana, U.S.
Died: November 20, 1942, Baltimore, Maryland, U.S.

## Abraham Lincoln

Lincoln was an American politician and lawyer who served as the 16th President of the United States from March 1861 until his assassination in April 1865. Lincoln led the United States through its Civil War. This war proved to be The United States' deadliest war and its greatest  moral, constitutional, and political crisis. In doing so, he sustained the Union, abolished slavery, strengthened the federal government, and modernized the economy. Famously born in a one-room log cabin, he went on to teach himself law while working as a farmer and store-keeper before successfully running for state office.

Born: February 12, 1809, Hodgenville, KY
Died: April 15, 1865, Washington D.C.

## Titus Livy

Titus Livius Patavinus was a Roman historian. He wrote a monumental history of Rome and the Roman people, 'Ab Urbe Condita Libri (Books from the Foundation of the City)', covering the period from the earliest legends of Rome before the traditional foundation in 753 BC through to his own lifetime. Growing up in a time of civil war, one modern translator has said of him that '"he was by nature a recluse, mild in temperament and averse to violence; the restorative peace of his time gave him the opportunity to turn all his imaginative passion to the legendary and historical past of the country he loved."

Born: 64 or 59 BC
Died: AD 12 or 17

## David Lloyd George

Lloyd George, 1st Earl Lloyd-George of Dwyfor, was a British statesman, solicitor, and was known for his vicious wit. Lloyd George was one of the most celebrated reforming chancellors of the 20th century and prime minister from 1916 to 1922. He was a key figure in the introduction of many reforms which laid the foundations of the modern welfare state. The only British prime minister to have been a native Welsh speaker, he was voted the third greatest British prime minister of the 20th century in a poll of 139 academics, and in 2002 he was named among the 100 Greatest Britons following a UK-wide vote.

Born: January 17, 1863, Chorlton-on-Medlock, United Kingdom
Died: March 26, 1945, Llanystumdwy, United Kingdom

## Vince Lombardi Jr.

Vincent Thomas "Vince" Lombardi was an American football player, coach, and executive in the National Football League (NFL). He is best known as the head coach of the Green Bay Packers during the 1960's, where he led the team to three straight and five total NFL Championships in seven years, in addition to winning the first two Super Bowls following the 1966 and 1967 NFL seasons. Lombardi is considered by many to be one of the best and most successful coaches in professional football history. The NFL's Super Bowl trophy is named in his honor.

Born: June 11, 1913, Brooklyn, New York City, NY
Died: September 3, 1970, Washington, D.C.

## Henry Wadsworth Longfellow

Longfellow was an American poet, novelist and educator. His mother was the daughter of a Revolutionary War hero, and his father was a member of Congress. After stints as professor at Bowdoin and later at Harvard College, he retired to concentrate on writing and lived most of his life in a former Revolutionary War headquarters of George Washington in Cambridge, Massachusetts. His lyric poetry contained much experimentation, though he also wrote in classical European forms. He became the most popular American poet in his own lifetime

Born Portland, Maine February 27, 1807
Died -Cambridge, Massachusetts, March 24, 1882

## Jim Lovell

James Arthur "Jim" Lovell Jr. is a former NASA astronaut, fighter jet test pilot, and retired captain in the United States Navy. He is mainly well known as the commander of the Apollo 13 mission, which suffered a massive failure during a mission to the Moon, but managed to get back unharmed to Earth by the resourceful efforts of the crew and mission control. The son of a oal furnace salesman, he is one of only 24 people to have flown to the Moon and the first of only three people to fly to the Moon twice as well as the only one to have flown there twice without making a landing. Lovell was the first person to fly in space four times.

Born: March 25, 1928, Cleveland, OH

## Clare Boothe Luce

Luce was an American author, playwright, Vanity Fair managing editor, two term congressperson, and U.S. Ambassador. She was the first American woman appointed to a significant ambassadorial post overseas. Early in her life she was extremely active in the Suffrage movement. Her remarkable life included experimenting with LSD. She was also a fervent anti-communist conservative, a war correspondent who endured bombing raids, and a long-term campaigner for the Republican party. She was the first female member of Congress to be awarded the Presidential Medal of Freedom.

Born: March 10, 1903, New York City, NY
Died: October 9, 1987, Washington, D.C.

## Jack Ma

Ma Yun, known professionally as Jack Ma, is a Chinese billionaire business mogul who is the founder and executive chairman of Alibaba Group, a group of successful Internet based businesses. Jack Ma's early life is riddled with disappointment, failures and setbacks. He used the lessons from his failures to create the powerhouse company Alibaba. As of 2018 he is one of China's richest men with a net worth of US$38.6 billion, and one of the wealthiest people in the world. He was ranked 2nd in the annual "World's 50 Greatest Leaders" list in2017 by Fortune. He currently devotes most of his time to education and philanthropy.

Born: September 10, 1964, Hangzhou, China

## Douglas MacArthur

Douglas MacArthur was a larger than life, controversial American five-star Army general. He was Chief of Staff of the United States Army during the 1930s and played a prominent role in the Pacific theater during World War II. He showed early promise while at the US Military Academy at West Point, and graduated first in his class. During World War I he proved himself to be a talented and courageous officer. He is most famous for returning to liberate the Philippines in 1944 after it had fallen to the Japanese. MacArthur led the United Nations forces during the beginning of the Korean War.

Born: January 26, 1880, Little Rock, AR
Died: April 5, 1964, MD

## Niccolò Machiavelli

Machiavelli was an Italian Renaissance historian, politician, diplomat, philosopher, humanist, and writer. He has often been called the founder of modern political science. He wrote poetry and songs and published correspondence. From an old aristocratic family, Machiavelli lived in a time of discord and war, with Spain, France and the Holy Roman Empire all fighting each other and the Pope. Appointed a diplomat at the time of the brutal Cesare Borgia, he quickly learned about the realpolitik of his day, which he set out in his most famous work, The Prince.

Born May 3, 1469, Florence, Italy
Died: June 21, 1527

### Harvey MacKay

Mackay is a businessman, author and syndicated columnist. When he was 26, he bought a small, failing envelope company which has grown to over a $100 million business employing over 600 people. His inspirational business books have sold over 10 million copies worldwide. He started volunteering with the American Cancer Society in Minnesota after his mother died from cancer, later becoming the Society's state chairman. He received the Outstanding Volunteer Fundraising Award in 1982 from the Association of Fundraising Professionals, Minnesota Chapter and the University of Minnesota Outstanding Achievement Award in 2008.

Born: 1932, Saint Paul, MN

**David Mahoney**

Mahoney was an American entrepreneur, marketing executive, philanthropist and author who spent years at Avis, Canada Dry and Colgate-Palmolive. He served in the army during World War II. Mahoney was an adviser to U.S. Presidents Nixon, Carter and Reagan  Later in life he turned his attention to promoting research in neuroscience. He founded the Dana Alliance for Brain Initiatives, a foundation organization of about 190 neuroscientists, with the purpose of educating the public about their field. He endowed programs in neuroscience at Harvard and at the University of Pennsylvania.

May 17, 1923, Bronx, NY
Died: May 1, 2000, Palm Beach, FL

**Nelson Mandela**

Nelson Rolihlahla Mandela was a South African who fought for and led the emancipation of South Africa from white minority rule and went on to serve as the country's first black president. He was an anti-apartheid revolutionary, politician, and activist, who served as President of South Africa from 1994 to 1999.  He spent 27 years in prison as a result of his actions to end apartheid. After he was freed in 1990, he negotiated the end of apartheid in South Africa and helped to begin the process of healing a racially divided country.  He then went on to spend the rest of his life fighting for human rights around the world.

Born: July 18, 1918, Mvezo, South Africa
Died: December 5, 2013, Johannesburg, South Africa

## Horace Mann

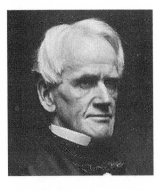

Mann was an American education reformer, politician, and the first great advocate of public education in order to preserve the republic. Despite growing up in poverty, and being mostly self-educated, he went on to help create a universal education system. It was said of him that "no-one did more than he to establish in the minds of the American people the conception that education should be universal, non-sectarian, free, and that its aims should be social efficiency, civic virtue, and character, rather than mere learning or the advancement of education ends."

Born May 4, 1796, Franklin, Mass., U.S.
Died Aug. 2, 1859, Yellow Springs, Ohio

### Ammianus Marcellinus

Marcellinus was a Greek Roman soldier, and historian, who wrote one of the very last major historical accounts that have survived from antiquity. He served with the legions in Gaul and Persia. after military service, he spent the rest of his life in Rome, where he wrote his 'Res Gestae', of which 18 out of 36 books survive. It constitutes the foundation of modern understanding of the history of the fourth century Roman Empire. It is a clear, comprehensive, and generally impartial account of events by a contemporary, though lacking in literary flair. Edward Gibbon called him "an accurate and faithful guide, who composed the history of his own times without indulging the prejudices and passions which usually affect the mind of a contemporary,"

Born: 330 AD, Antioch, Turkey
Died: 395 AD, Rome

409

## Richard "Dick" Marcinko

Richard "Dick" Marcinko is a former United States Navy officer, retired U.S. Navy SEAL commander and highly decorated Vietnam War veteran. He was the first commanding officer of SEAL Team Six, the Navy's anti-terrorist group and Red Cell, a high-level anti-terrorist unit. His father was Croat from Dubrava near Stolac in Bosnia and Herzegovina and his mother was a Romanian from Slovakia. After retiring from the United States Navy, he became an author, radio talk show host, military consultant, and motivational speaker. Marcinko was convicted of conspiracy to defraud the government on January 24, 1990 and sentenced to 21 months in federal prison.

Born: November 21, 1940 Lansford, PA

## George Catlett Marshall, Jr

George Catlett Marshall, Jr. was an American statesman and soldier. He was Chief of Staff of the United States Army under presidents Franklin D. Roosevelt and Harry S. Truman. After World War II, the European economy was in disarray. Marshall thought that it was in the United States' best interest for Europe to be economically secure. In June of 1947, Marshall developed a comprehensive economic recovery program, which would eventually be called the Marshall Plan, which would eliminate trade barriers, rejuvenate industry and make Europe flourish again. The plan was a resounding success.

Born: December 31, 1880, Uniontown, PA
Died: October 16, 1959, Washington, D.C.

## The Emperor Maurice

Maurice, Latin in full Mauricius Flavius Tiberius, was a renowned general and emperor of the Byzantine Empire who helped reconstruct the shattered late Eastern Rome into a reinvigorated and organized empire. He defeated the Persians, ending an era of financial tribute, reaffirmed Constantinople's rule over North Africa, halted the advance of the Lombards, took military control over the Caucasus, and campaigned over the Danube. The Strategikon, a manual of war which influenced European and Middle Eastern military traditions for well over a millennium, is traditionally attributed to Maurice.

Born: 539 AD, Arabissus
Died: November 27, 602 AD, Constantinople

## Dr. Charles Mayo

Charles Horace Mayo was an American medical practitioner and was one of the founders of the Mayo Clinic. Born into a medical family, Mayo graduated from Northwestern University in 1888 and joined the family practice. This became he not-for-profit Mayo Clinic in 1919, and came to be regarded as one of the foremost medical treatment and research institutions in the world. Mayo himself specialized in surgery of the thyroid and nervous system. He and early partners insisted on sterile conditions in the operating room, and that was one of many factors which contributed to the practice's early surgical successes.

Born: July 19, 1865
Died: May 26, 1939

**Mencius**

Mencius or Mengzi was a Chinese
philosopher, better known in China as
"Master Meng." He is the most famous
Confucian after Confucius himself.
Foremost among his basic principles
was an emphasis on the responsibility of
rulers to provide for the common people.
He led the life of an itinerant sage, travelling throughout China for
four decades trying to encourage rulers to reform. While Confucius
himself did not explicitly focus on the subject of human nature,
Mencius asserted the innate goodness of the individual, believing that
it was society's influence that caused bad moral character.

Born: 372 BCE, Zoucheng, China
Died: 289 BCE

**Donald H. McGannon**

McGannon was a broadcasting industry
executive during the formative years
of the television industry in the United
States. He was a devoted advocate of
broadcasting's potential for good and
worked to improve the standards of radio
and television broadcasting. A graduate of
Fordham law School, he practised law for several years before becoming
General Manager and Assistant Director of the DuMont Television
Network. A vocal advocate of social responsibility in broadcasting,
he worked to educate the public through television, and successfully
managed to remove cigarette advertising from his own station.

Born: September 9, 1920, New York City, NY
Died: May 23, 1984, Chester, CT

## George J. Mecherle

George Jacob "G.J." Mecherle was a farmer who founded State Farm Insurance, after becoming frustrated with the insurance rates charged to farmers. Moving from farming to selling tractors, he found that he had a knack of selling to farmers, partly because he was one himself. This and the way non-farmers were extorting insurance money convinced him that a company run by farmers for farmers would succeed. Eventually, his company became the largest property and casualty insurer in the United States and one of the 20 largest corporations on the Fortune 500.

Born: June 7, 1877, Merna, Illinois, IL
Died: March 10, 1951, Bloomington, IL

## Golda Meir

Golda Meir was the fourth elected Prime Minister of Israel, and the only woman to ever be the Prime Minister. She was elected Prime Minister of Israel after serving as Minister of Labor and Foreign Minister. Born in Kiev, she immigrated to the USA, then to Palestine in 1921. Travelling to the USA in 1948, she was able to secure $50,000,000 to buy arms to enforce the terrible Palestinian Catastrophe, slaughtering the innocents and driving families from their homes into refugee camps. She continued to be an 'Iron Lady' until her death, presiding over the Yom Kippur War that annexed the Golan Heights.

Born: May 3, 1898, Kiev, Ukraine
Died: December 8, 1978, Jerusalem

### Helmuth Karl Bernhard Graf von Moltke

Helmuth Graf von Moltke was a German army field marshall credited with modernizing the military through the use of improved troop movement and placement in battle. His military colleagues called him "The Golden Man," due to his reputation for integrity, and decency. He is considered to be one of the most brilliant military strategists of the 1800's. The chief of staff of the Prussian Army for thirty years, he was described as embodying "Prussian military organization and tactical genius."

Born: 26 October 26, 1800, Parchim, Duchy of Mecklenburg-Schwerin, Holy Roman Empire
Died April 24, 1891, Berlin, Kingdom of Prussia, German Empire

### Bernard Montgomery

British Field Marshall Bernard Law Montgomery (nicknamed "Monty" and the "Spartan General") was one of the most decorated military officers of World War II. Montgomery was the senior British officer on D-Day and his stubborn persistence that invasion forces be enlarged from three to eight divisions was essential to the Allies' success. During World War I, he was shot through the right lung by a sniper. He was revered by the men in his command in part because he went above and beyond to take care of them. He served as NATO's Deputy Supreme Allied Commander Europe until his retirement.

Born: 17 November 17, 1887 – Kennington, Surrey, England
Died 24 March 24, 1976, Alton, Hampshire, England

# J. P. Morgan

John Pierpont "J. P." Morgan was an American financier and one of the most powerful bankers of the late 19th and early 20th Century. He co-founded the firm, J.P. Morgan & Company, which was a predecessor the modern-day financial juggernaut JPMorgan Chase. arranged the merger of Edison General Electric and Thomson-Houston Electric Company to form General Electric. He also played important roles in the formation of the United States Steel Corporation, International Harvester and AT&T. He also directed the banking coalition that stopped the Panic of 1907.

Born: April 17, 1837, Hartford, Connecticut, U.S.
Died: March 31, 1913 Rome, Italy

## Audie Murphy

Murphy was the most decorated U.S. soldier of World War II, including the military's highest award, the Congressional Medal of Honor. Despite being rejected for service by the Marines, and the Navy, because of his youth and size, Murphy was determined to get into the fight. Desperate to go fight for his country, at the age of 16 he lied about his age, claimed he was 18 and enlisted in the Army. After the war he became a successful actor in Westerns, and played himself in the 1955 film 'To Hell and Back'. His later years were plagued by Post Traumatic Stress Disorder and an addiction to sleeping pills.

Born: June 20, 1925, Kingston, TX-
Died: May 28, 1971, Catawba, VA

415

**Miyamoto Musashi**

Legendary Samurai, and considered the greatest swordsman to ever live, Miyamoto Bennosuke was an expert Japanese swordsman and rōnin (a masterless Samurai). Musashi, as he was most commonly known, became renowned through stories of his exceptional and singular double bladed swordsmanship style, and undefeated record in his sixty duels. He was the founder of the Hyōhō Niten Ichi-ryū or Niten-ryū style of swordsmanship and in his final years authored The Book of Five Rings, a book on strategy, tactics, and philosophy that is still studied today.

Born: 1584, Harima Province, Japan
Died: June 13, 1645, Higo Province, Japan

**Elon Musk**

South African serial entrepreneur, polymath, and billionaire Elon Reeve Musk is the founder, CEO, and CTO of SpaceX; co-founder, CEO, and product architect of Tesla Motors; co-founder and chairman of SolarCity; co-chairman of OpenAI. He made his initial fortune when his startup Zip2 was acquired and he walked away with $22 Million. He later went on to co-found X2 which eventually merged with another start up that became PayPal. He taught himself computer programming at the age of 10, and by the age of 12 sold the code of a BASIC-based video game he created called Blastar for approximately $500. Today he has a net worth of $22.8 billion.

Born June 28, 1971, Pretoria, South Africa

## Joe Namath

Joseph William Namath nicknamed "Broadway Joe," is a former American football quarterback and actor. Namath is most famous for making an audacious claim before Super Bowl III, "We're going to win the game. I guarantee it." He retired from football, after playing in 143 games over a span of 13 years in the AFL and NFL He started his television career by guest-starring as himself, before going on to star on Broadway. Born in the steelworking community of Pennsylvania to parents of Hungarian descent, Namath excelled in all sports throughout his formative years. His autobiography chronicles his long-term struggle with alcohol.

Born: May 31, 1943, Beaver Falls, PA

## Napoleon I

Napoleon Bonaparte, also known as Napoleon I, was a French military genius, and emperor who conquered most of Europe in the early 19th century. Napoleon rocketed through the ranks of the military during the French Revolution (1789-1799) to become Emperor of the French in 1804. He is considered to be one of the greatest military commanders in history. Launching a series of wars across mainland Europe, he won most of these wars and the vast majority of his battles, building a large empire that ruled over continental Europe before its final collapse in 1815.

Born: August 15, 1769, Ajaccio, France
Died: May 5, 1821, Longwood House, Island of St. Helena, UK

## Charlton Ogburn

Ogburn was a journalist and author of memoirs and non-fiction works, and a one-time member of a special U.S. Army unit called Merrill's Marauders. The special unit was officially designated as the "5307th Composite Unit (Provisional)" Code Name: "GALAHAD," they would later become known as "Merrill's Marauders" named after its leader, Brigadier General Frank Merrill. They engaged in long range penetration special operations jungle warfare and fought in the South-East Asian theater of World War II. In later years he wrote books and magazine articles, and was a Shakespeare scholar.

Born: 15 March 1911 Charlton Ogburn GA
Died: 19 October 1998 Beaufort, SC

## Onasander

Onasander or Onosander was a Greek philosopher best known for his book Strategikos, which was a treatise on the skills of being a great general. A Platonic philosopher, he dedicated his work The General to the Roman Veranius, who was a consul in 49 CE. The work deals in plain style with the sort of morals and social and military qualities and attitudes expeted of a virtuous and militarily successful general. It is also concerned with such matters as his choice of staff; attitude to war; religious duties; military formations; conduct in allied and hostile lands; difficult terrains; camps; drill; spies; guards; deserters; battle formations and maneuvers; and other matters, ending with conduct after victory. To this day it remains the best source of information on ancient Greek military tactics,especially light infantry tactics, and provides information not commonly available in other ancient works.

Lived 1st century AD

## William Oncken Jr.

Oncken was an American organizational planning and management expert. He worked under Dr. H. D. Smythe on the Manhattan Project, and as a Naval officer at the Naval Ordnance Laboratory in Washington DC. At the war's end, he interviewed his counterparts in the Japanese military to document their technical advances during the War. In 1947 he worked at the Pentagon holding a series of high level positions. In 1956 he was in charge of organizational planning and development for a leading east coast corporation. Oncken was a regular lecturer in general management at leading universities from coast to coast, and was a popular keynote speaker at national conventions. He was also a faculty member of the National University of the Young Presidents Organization.

Born Buffalo, NY, 1912
Died 1988

## George Orwell

Eric Arthur Blair, better known by the pen name George Orwell, was an English novelist, essayist, journalist, and critic. A lifelong humanitarian and democratic socialist, he is best known for his chilling book '1984', set in a totalitarian future. His other important works include 'Animal Farm', his autobiographical account of the Spanish Civil War 'Homage to Catalonia', and many books and essays about working class life and social justice. In 2008, The Times ranked him second on a list of "The 50 greatest British writers since 1945".

Born: June 25, 1903, Motihari, India
Died: January 21, 1950, London, United Kingdom

## Larry Page

Lawrence "Larry" Edward Page is an American Internet entrepreneur and computer scientist who co-founded Google with Sergey Brin. Page is the chief executive officer of Google's parent company, Alphabet Inc. His father was a computer science professor at Michigan State University where his mother was an instructor in computer programming. In an interview, Page recalled that his childhood, house "was usually a mess, with computers, science, and technology magazines and Popular Science magazines all over the place. For his doctorate thesis he explored the mathematical properties of the World Wide Web, understanding its link structure as a huge graph.

Born: March 26, 1973, East Lansing, MI

## Lucius Aemilius Paulus

Also known as Paulus Lucius Aemilius Paullus Macedonicus was a two-time consul of the Roman Republic and a renown general who conquered Macedon. Paulus's return to Rome was glorious. In the Third Macedonian War he won the decisive Battle of Pydna. With the immense plunder collected in Macedonia and Epirus, he celebrated a spectacular triumph, featuring no less than the captured king of Macedonia himself, and the king's sons, putting an end to the Antigonid dynasty. As a gesture of acknowledgement, the Senate awarded him the nickname Macedonicus.

Born: 229 BCE, Rome, Italy
Died: 160 BCE, Rome, Italy

## Thomas Paine

Thomas Paine was an English-American revolutionary, political theorist, activist, and philosopher. In 1776, Paine wrote a pamphlet called "Common Sense," that helped mold many of the ideas that highlighted during the Revolutionary years. Deeply involved in the French Revolution, he wrote the hugely influential 'Rights of Man' in part as a defense of the Revolution against its critics. A writ being issued for his arrest in early 1792, Paine fled to France, but was arrested and imprisoned. In 1802, he returned to the U.S. where he died on June 8, 1809. Only six people attended his funeral.

Born: February 9, 1737, Thetford, United Kingdom
Died: June 8, 1809, Greenwich Village, New York City, NY

## Blaise Pascal

Pascal was a French mathematician, physicist, inventor, religious philosopher, tax collector, mathematics genius. and master of prose. He laid the groundwork for the modern theory of probabilities. He was a child prodigy who was home schooled by his father. He wrote a significant treatise on the subject of projective geometry at the age of 16, and later corresponded with Pierre de Fermat on probability theory, strongly influencing the development of modern economics and social science. He wrote down his thoughts about life, death and the world in his most famous work, Pensées.

Born: June 19, 1623, Clermont-Ferrand, France
Died: August 19, 1662, Paris, France

## George S. Patton

George Smith Patton Jr. was a General of the United States Army who is best known for his leadership of the U.S. Third Army in France and Germany following the Allied invasion of Normandy in June 1944. Known as "Old Blood and Guts" by his troops, he was a great military strategist and tactician. He graduated from the U.S. Military Academy at West Point in 1909 and experienced his first taste of battle in 1915, when he was assigned to lead cavalry troops against Mexican forces led by Pancho Villa along the U.S.-Mexico border. Under his decisive leadership the Third Army won the Battle of the Bulge.

Born: November 11, 1885, San Gabriel, CA
Died: December 21, 1945, Heidelberg, Germany

## Pericles

Pericles was a distinguished and influential Greek statesman, brilliant general, orator, patron of the arts and politician during the "Golden Age" of Greece. Pericles had such a profound influence on Athenian society that Thucydides, a contemporary historian, acclaimed him as "the first citizen of Athens". Pericles led his countrymen during the first two years of the Peloponnesian War. The period during which he led Athens, roughly from 461 to 429 BC, is sometimes known as the "Age of Pericles". Builder of the Parthenon, it was through his efforts that Athens became the centre of Greek civilisation.

Born: 498 BCE, Holargos, Greece
Died: 429 BCE, Athens, Greece

# Eva Perón

María Eva Duarte de Perón, better known as Eva Peron and Evita, served as the First Lady of Argentina from 1946 until her death in 1952. She became an influential political figure with a massive base of support among the poor and working class. She inspired millions with her campaigns to help the poor and give women the right to vote. She was revered by her supporters because of her efforts to end poverty and injustice. She died as a result of fast moving cancer, though a lobotomy that her husband forced upon Eva in order to control her may have killed her sooner than the cancer would have.

Born: May 7, 1919, Los Toldos, Argentina
Died: July 26, 1952, Buenos Aires, Argentina

# H. Ross Perot

Henry Ross Perot, known as Ross Perot, is an American billionaire computer businessman best known for being an independent presidential candidate in 1992 against George H.W. Bush and Bill Clinton. He served four years as a naval officer after graduating from the U.S. Naval Academy at Annapolis. He went on to become one of IBM's top sales people. With a $1,000 loan from his wife, Perot founded Electronic Data Systems (EDS). EDS went on to become a multi-billion dollar company. In 2009, Dell acquired Perot Systems for $3.9 billion. perot himself has an estimated net worth of about $4.1 billion.

Born: June 27, 1930, Texarkana, TX

## John "Black Jack" Pershing

John Joseph "Black Jack" Pershing was a United States Army general. He was the only American to be promoted during his own lifetime to General of the Armies rank, the highest possible rank in the United States Army. His iron discipline caused him to be respected and hated by the soldiers in his command. He is most famous as the commander of the American Expeditionary Force on the Western Front in World War I, 1917–18. His reliance on costly frontal assaults, long after other Allied armies had abandoned such tactics, has been blamed for causing unnecessarily high American casualties

Born: September 13, 1860, Laclede, MO
Died: July 15, 1948, Washington, D.C.

## Peter the Great

Peter the Great, Peter I, full name Peter Alexeyevich was the Tsar of Russia and later the Russian Empire from May 7, 1682 until his death, jointly ruling before 1696 with his older half-brother, Ivan V Alekseyevich. As the Renaissance and the Reformation spread through Europe, Russia was still considered severely underdeveloped. Peter overcame violent opposition from the country's medieval aristocracy and initiated a series of reforms extensive reforms in an attempt to reestablish Russia as an important nation. He was one of Russia's greatest statesmen, organizers, and reformers.

Born: June 9, 1672, Moscow, Russia
Died: February 8, 1725, Saint Petersburg, Russia

## Don Peterson

Ford Motor Company CEO Donald Eugene Peterson was credited for turning Ford around from a money losing company to one whose profits surpassed those of General Motors for the first time in sixty years. Born in Pipestone, Minnesota, Petersen served in the U.S. Marine Corps in World War II and the Korean War. He went on to spend over 40 years working for the Ford company. His sucesses made him a "Most Valuable Person" of 1988 for USA Today and "CEO of the Year" for Chief Executive magazine in 1989. Petersen is said to have transformed Ford with his inclusive, team-oriented management style.

Born: September 4, 1926, Pipestone, MN

## T. Boone Pickens

Thomas Boone Pickens, Jr., known as T. Boone Pickens, is a self-made American business tycoon, financier, and philanthropist. He became famous in the 1980's as a corporate raider. He is currently chairman of the hedge fund BP Capital Management. Most recently, Pickens has focused on promoting his "Pickens Plan" to boost adoption of wind, solar, and especially natural gas. Pickens has a net worth of $500 million, but could have been a billionaire; he has has contributed significantly to philanthropic projects, particularly supporting his old college Oklahoma State University with $500 million, as well as giving to the Hurricane Katrina relief programme.

Born: May 22, 1928, Holdenville, OK

## Plato

Plato was a Greek philosopher, a teacher of Aristotle, and a student of Socrates. He founded the Academy in Athens, Greece, which is thought to be the first university in the Western world. The Stanford Encyclopedia of Philosophy describes Plato as "...one of the most dazzling writers in the Western literary tradition and one of the most penetrating, wide-ranging, and influential authors in the history of philosophy. Few other authors in the history of Western philosophy approximate him in depth and range: perhaps only Aristotle, Aquinas and Kant would be generally agreed to be of the same rank."

Born c. 428 BCE
Died Athens, Greece, c. 348 BCE

## Plutarch

Plutarch, later Lucius Mestrius Plutarchus, was a prolific Greek biographer who wrote extensively about Greek and Roman culture. He was best known for his biographies of dominant figures in ancient times and his writing on ethics and virtue. He is credited with over 227 works. His most well-known work, Bioi Parallēloi (Parallel Lives), is a collection of biographies of famous Greek and Roman warriors, politicians, brilliant orators, and statesmen. Born into a wealthy family, he worked as a magistrate and ambassador before spending the last thirty years of his life as a priest in Delphi.

Born: 45 AD, Chaeronea, Greece
Died: 120 AD, Delphi, Greece

## Polybius

Polybius was a Greek statesman, cavalry commander, and historian who wrote 40 books on the rise of Rome. Detained for 17 years as a hostage in Rome, he became acquainted with all the great families of the day. On his release he decided not to return home, but isntead traveled the Mediterranean fact-finding and interviewing veterans. Polybius is important for his analysis of the mixed constitution or the separation of powers in government, which was influential on Montesquieu's The Spirit of the Laws and on the creators of the United States Constitution.

Born c. 200 BCE, Megalopolis, Arcadia, Greece
Died c. BCE 118

## Pierre-Joseph Proudhon

Proudhon was a French political philosopher who was the first person to call himself an "anarchist" and is one of the first anarchist thinkers. Proudhon's notion of revolution did not entail violence against the prevailing system or civil war, but rather called for the complete transformation of society. He was the originator of the phrase 'Property is theft' which later became associated with Karl Marx, with whom he corresponded, but the two fell out. Asserting that 'Anarchy is order without power', Proudhon believed that peaceful social revolution was both possible and necessary.

Born: January 15, 1809, Besançon, France
Died: January 19, 1865, Passy, Paris, France

## Mujibur Rahman

Sheikh Mujibur Rahman was a Bengali politician and statesman who was the founding leader of the People's Republic of Bangladesh. He is revered in Bangladesh as the founding father of the nation, and served as the first President, and later as the Prime Minister. His government enacted a constitution proclaiming socialism and secular democracy. However, he faced challenges of rampant unemployment, poverty, and corruption. He initiated one party socialist rule in January 1975. Six months later he and most of his family were assassinated by a group of junior army officers.

Born: March 17, 1920, Tungipara Upazila, Bangladesh
Died: August 15, 1975, Dhaka, Bangladesh

## Jeannette Rankin

Jeannette Pickering Rankin was the first woman elected to the Congress of the United States. She was elected to the U.S. House of Representatives by the state of Montana in 1916, and again in 1940 , both times coinciding with the outbreak of World War. She was a pacifist and suffragette who tirelessly worked as a social activist. She voted against war in 1917 and was the only member of Congress to vote against declaring war on Japan after the attack on Pearl Harbor in 1941. She initiated the legislation that eventually became the 19th Constitutional Amendment, granting full voting rights to women.

Born: June 11, 1880, Missoula County, Montana, MT
Died: May 18, 1973, Carmel-by-the-Sea, CA

## Ronald Reagan

Ronald Reagan was the 40th U.S. president (1981 to 1989), governor of California (1967 to 1975). Reagan was called the "Great Communicator." He reduced taxes, exploded defense spending, negotiated a nuclear arms reduction agreement with the Soviet Union, and is credited with bringing an end to the Cold War. Born into a poor family, he became an actor, and starred in a small number of roles. Becoming President of the Screen Actors Guild he worked against the perceived threat of communiam. Reagan survived a 1981 assassination attempt, and died at age 93 of Alzheimer's disease.

Born: February 6, 1911, Tampico, IL
Died: June 5, 2004, Bel-Air, Los Angeles, CA

## Loretta "Lori" Reynolds

Marine Major General Loretta "Lori" Reynolds is a Lieutenant General in the United States Marine Corps, the third woman to earn that rank in the Marines. Reynolds assumed command of the 9th Communication Battalion on June 8, 2003. She deployed in support of Operation Iraqi Freedom to Fallujah, Iraq in February 2004. During this deployment she was responsible for providing communications and IT support. Her no-nonsense leadership style was instrumental in the success of the battalion's mission. During this time she led from the front and visited her Marines at outlying camps to personally check on their welfare.

## Eddie Rickenbacker

Edward Vernon Rickenbacker was a successful race car driver, fighter pilot, airline executive, and distinguished statesman. He raced three times in the Indianapolis 500, and during World War I became America's most successful fighter ace. He went on to become president of
Eastern Airlines until World War II began. In 1942, while flying in a B-17, the plane ran out of fuel, and went down in the Pacific. Rickenbacker and seven other men, floated in a raft for twenty-two days before they were rescued. One man died, and Rickenbacker, the oldest in the raft, lost 60 pounds.

Born: October 8, 1890, Columbus, OH
Died: July 23, 1973, Zürich, Switzerland

## Erwin Rommel

Johannes Erwin Eugen Rommel, known as the Desert Fox, was a brilliant Field Marshal in the German army during World War II. Rommel was one of German's most respected and popular generals during World War II, and gained the respect of his enemies due to his
impressive victories. His soldiers held him in reverence due to his style of leading from the front rather than the rear as most generals did. In 1944, he was implicated in a plot to assassinate Hitler. To save his family and staff from arrest, persecution, and torture, Rommel chose to take a cyanide pill, as ordered by Nazi officers.

Born: November 15, 1891, Heidenheim an der Brenz, Germany
Died: October 14, 1944, Herrlingen, Germany

## Eleanor Roosevelt

Anna Eleanor Roosevelt was an American politician, diplomat, and activist. She was the longest-serving First Lady of the United States, having held the post from March 1933 to April 1945. She served as United States Delegate to the United Nations General Assembly from 1945 to 1952, and in 1946 was a dynamic force behind the U.N.'s Declaration of Human Rights. She is remembered as a champion for the common person. One of the most esteemed women in the world, President Harry S. Truman called her the "First Lady of the World" in tribute to her human rights achievements.

Born: October 11, 1884, New York City, NY
Died: November 7, 1962, Manhattan, NY

## Franklin D. Roosevelt

Franklin Delano Roosevelt, commonly known as FDR, was an American statesman and transformational political leader who, despite being stricken with polio, was the 32nd President of the United States from 1933 until his death in 1945. He became president during the Great Depression and helped to enact legislation that stabilized the economy. His first terms of office promoted the New Deal, a variety of programs designed to produce relief, recovery, and reform. Re-elected in 1940, his final years were taken up with the Second World War, as a leader of the Allies.

Born: January 30, 1882, Hyde Park, NY
Died: April 12, 1945, Warm Springs, GA

## Theodore Roosevelt

Roosevelt was an American statesman, author, explorer, soldier, naturalist and reformer who served as the 26th President of the United States from 1901 to 1909. During the Spanish-American War, Roosevelt was lieutenant colonel of the Rough Rider Regiment, which he led on a charge at the battle of San Juan. He was one of the most conspicuous heroes of the war. He saw the role of the President as a "steward of the people" who should do whatever he could for the public good unless specifically forbidden by law or the Constitution. Roosevelt is generally ranked as one of the five best presidents.

Born: October 27, 1858, Manhattan, New York City, NY
Died: January 6, 1919, Sagamore Hill, Town of Oyster Bay, NY

## Rumi

Jalāl ad-Dīn Muhammad Rūmī, more popularly simply as Rumi, was a 13th-century Persian poet, jurist, and Sufi master. His poems have been widely translated into many of the world's languages and transposed into various formats. Rumi's major work is the Spiritual Couplets, a six-volume poem considered by many to be one of the greatest works of mystical poetry and regarded by some Sufis as the Persian-language Qur'an. On his death, his followers and his son Sultan Walad founded the Mevlevi Order, also known as the Order of the Whirling Dervishes.

Born: September 30, 1207, Balkh Province, Afghanistan
Died: December 17, 1273, Konya, Turkey

## Bertrand Russell

Bertrand Arthur William Russell was a Welsh philosopher, social critic, reformer, mathematician, logician, historian, and pacifist. He was considered one of the foremost philosophers of the 20th century. He was imprisoned in 1918 for anti-war views on World War I, and again in 1961 for his involvement in an anti-nuclear weapons protest. One of the foremost philosophers and logicians of his day, he is considered one of the founders of analytic philosophy, and a major influence on modern thought. A prolific author, Russell was awarded the Nobel Prize in Literature in 1950.

Born: 18 May 1872 in Ravenscroft, Trelleck, Monmouthshire, Wales
Died: 2 February 1970 in Penrhyndeudraeth, Merioneth, Wales

## Sadhguru

Sadhguru. Jaggi Vasudev, more commonly known as Sadhguru, is a former entrepreneur, and the founder of the Isha Foundation, a non-profit organization which offers Yoga programs around the world. He has spoken before the World Economic Forum several times on diverse issues such as the environment, economic development and education. His foundation launched Project GreenHands which is a grassroots ecological initiative that has planted over of 25 million trees across India. Sadhguru was given the Padma Vibhushan civilian award by the Government of India in 2017 in recognition of his contribution to the field of spiritualism.

Born: September 3, 1957, Mysore, India

## Carl Sagan

Carl Edward Sagan was an American astronomer, cosmologist, astrophysicist, astro-biologist, science popularizer, and science communicator in astronomy and other natural sciences. He is particularly famous for narrating and co-writing the award-winning 1980 television series 'Cosmos: A Personal Voyage', the most widely watched series in the history of American public television. Sagan assembled the first physical messages sent into space, the Pioneer plaque and the Voyager Golden Record, universal messages that could potentially be understood by any extraterrestrial intelligence that might find them.

Born: November 9, 1934, Brooklyn, New York City, NY
Died: December 20, 1996, Seattle, WA

## Antoine de Saint-Exupery

Antoine Marie Jean-Baptiste Roger, Comte de Saint-Exupéry was a French writer, military aviator, poet, and journalist. He is best remembered for his novel The Little Prince. Saint-Exupéry was a successful commercial pilot flying airmail routes in Europe, Africa and South America until World War II, when he joined the French Air Force and flew reconnaissance missions against the Nazis. Though he was way past the maximum age, he flew spy missions for the resistance in North Africa. He disappeared without trace over the Mediterranean on a reconnaissance mission in July 1944.

Born: June 29, 1900, Lyon, France
Died: July 31, 1944, Marseille, France

## Sallust

Gaius Sallustius Crispus was a Roman Senator, soldier, and historian. Sallust is the earliest known Roman historian with surviving works to his name. The Sallustii were a provincial noble family of Sabine origin. They belonged to the equestrian order and had full Roman citizenship. From the beginning of his public career, Sallust operated as a partisan of Julius Caesar, to whom he owed political advancement. In 50 BC, the censor Appius Claudius Pulcher removed him from the Senate on the grounds of gross immorality (probably because of his opposition to Milo and Cicero). In the following year, perhaps through Caesar's influence, he was reinstated. Of his works, Martial stated: "Sallust, according to the judgment of the learned, will rank as the prince of Roman historiographers".

Born c. 86 BCE, Amiternum, Italy
Died 35 or34 BCE, Rome, Italy

## Herbert Louis Samuel

Herbert Louis Samuel, 1st Viscount Samuel, was a British statesman, party leader, diplomat and philosopher. He was one of the first Jewish members of the British cabinet (as chancellor of the duchy of Lancaster, 1909–10). He was the last member of the Liberal Party to hold one of the four Great Offices of State. One of his most important positions was as the first British High Commissioner for Palestine from 1920 until 1925. A a Zionist, the Morning Post said of him that "Sir Herbert Samuel's appointment as High Commissioner was regarded by everyone, except Jews, as a serious mistake."

Born Nov. 6, 1870, Liverpool, United Kingdom
Died Feb. 5, 1963, London, United Kingdom

### Ernest Henry Shackleton

Shackleton was a British explorer best known for his expeditions to Antarctica. He led three expeditions to the Antarctic, one of them coming within 179 km (111 mi) of reaching the South Pole which was the closest anyone had ever come at that time. Shackleton is most remembered for leading the legendary Endurance expedition to Antarctica, in which his men barely survived for ten months on ice floes and on a brutal, barren island after their ship was crushed and sunk by pack ice in the Weddell Sea in 1914. Away from his expeditions, Shackleton's life was generally restless and unfulfilled, and he died heavily in debt.

Born: February 15, 1874, Kilkea, Republic of Ireland
Died: January 5, 1922, Grytviken, South Georgia

### Howard Schultz

Schultz is an American businessman best known as the former CEO of Starbucks. He came from a struggling working class family and worked a string of jobs until at the age of 29 he was hired as the director of retail operations and marketing for Starbucks which at the time had only three stores. Schultz was named Fortune magazine's 2011 Businessperson of the Year for his initiatives in the economy and job market. In November 2017, the NAACP Legal Defense and Educational Fund presented Schultz with the National Equal Justice Award. Forbes magazine ranked Schultz as the 232nd richest person in the United States, with a net worth of $3.1 billion as of April 2017.

Born: July 19, 1953, Brooklyn, New York City, NY

## Carl Schurz

Carl Christian Schurz was a German-American political leader, revolutionary, reformer, orator, slavery abolitionist, journalist and soldier. As a young man, Schurz participated in the aborted German revolution of 1848, was jailed, escaped, and eventually made it to the U.S. In 1862, he joined the Union army and commanded troops during America's Civil War at the Second Battle of Bull Run, the battles of Chancellorsville, Gettysburg, and Chattanooga. After the Civil War he served as U.S. senator from 1869 to 1875, and sought to make civil service based on merit rather than political connections.

Born: March 2, 1829, Liblar, near Cologne, Prussia (now Germany)
Died: May 14, 1906, New York City, NY

## Charles M. Schwab

Michael Schwab was an American entrepreneur and steel magnate. He served as president of both the Carnegie Steel Company and United States Steel Corporation and later grew Bethlehem Steel into one of America's largest steel producers. He started as a stake-driver in the engineering corps of the Edgar Thomson Steel Works and Furnaces in Braddock, Pennsylvania. At only 35 he became president of the Carnegie Steel Company. In 1901, he helped negotiate the secret sale of Carnegie Steel to a group of New York–based financiers and became the first president of the U.S. Steel Corporation.

Born: February 18, 1862, Williamsburg, PA
Died: September 18, 1939, New York

### H. Norman Schwarzkopf, Jr.

Herbert Norman Schwarzkopf Jr. was a United States Army general. He commanded all coalition forces in the first Gulf War, also known as "Operation Desert Storm." He was a much-decorated combat soldier in Vietnam, being awarded three Silver Star Medals, two Purple Hearts, and the Legion of Merit. Schwarzkopf was known popularly as "Stormin' Norman" for his well-known explosive temper, though he preferred to be called "Bear," a nickname given to him by his troops. Schwarzkopf was considered an exceptional leader by many biographers.

Born August 22, 1934 in Trenton, New Jersey
Died December 27, 2012 in Tampa, Florida

### Albert Schweitzer

Schweitzer was a French-German physician, theologian, autodidact, and philosopher. As a music scholar and organist, he studied the music of Johann Sebastian Bach and influenced the Organ Reform Movement (Orgelbewegung). With his wife, he founded a hospital in Africa. He received the 1952 Nobel Peace Prize for his philosophy of "Reverence for Life", but it was later revealed that his hospital was squalid and did not come up to modern stadards, and was strongly criticised by African medical campaigners, while Schweitzer had little contact with the local people.

Born: January 14, 1875, Kaysersberg, now Haut-Rhin, France
Died: September 4, 1965, Lambaréné, Gabon

## Junior Seau

Tiaina Baul "Junior" Seau Jr. was a linebacker in the National Football League. Known for his consistently ferocious playing style, he was a 10-time All-Pro, 12-time Pro Bowl selection, and named to the NFL 1990s All-Decade Team. He is considered one of the best linebackers to ever play the game of football. Seau died by suicide by shooting himself in the chest in 2012 at the age of 43. Later studies concluded that Seau suffered from chronic traumatic encephalopathy, a type of brain damage that has also been found in other deceased former NFL players and other NFL players who have died by suicide.

Born: January 19, 1969, San Diego, CA
Died: May 2, 2012, Oceanside, CA

## Takeda Shingen

Shingen was a powerful Japanese samurai feudal lord with exceptional military prestige in the late stage of the Sengoku period during the mid-1500's. Born into a noble family, he was an accomplished poet in his youth. He won his first major victory at the Battle of Un no Kuchi while only 15. He took over his clan in a coup that deposed and exiled his father, then started expanding into the surrounding territories. By the time he was 49 years old he was one of the most powerful men in Japan, and the only one capable of defying unifyer Oda Nobunaga's attempt to be sole ruler, but died, some say by sniper, trying to do so.

Born: December 1, 1521 Kai Province, Japan
Died: May 13, 1573, Mikawa Province, Japan

## Sitting Bull

Sitting Bull was a Hunkpapa Lakota Native American chief and holy man who led his people during years of resistance to United States government policies. After a vision in which he saw many soldiers, "as thick as grasshoppers," falling upside down into the Lakota camp, he defeated General George Custer at the Battle at Little Bighorn, but was eventually forced to surrender. He was killed by Indian agency police on the Standing Rock Indian Reservation during an attempt to arrest him, at a time when authorities feared that he would join the Ghost Dance movement.

Born Grand River, South Dakota 1831
Died 1890 Grand River, South Dakota

## Socrates

Socrates was a Greek philosopher who is considered to be the founding figure of Western philosophy, although he left no written works of his own. He served with courage and distinction as a soldier before he embarked on the path of a philosopher. His unique method of teaching, what would eventually become known as the Socratic Method, entailed not giving knowledge but rather asking a myriad of questions until his students had an epiphany and came to their own conclusion. He took poison after he was tried and convinced for supposedly corrupting the youth, and "denying the Gods."

Born c. 470 BCE, Athens, Greece
Died 399 BCE, Athens, Greece

## Aleksandr Solzhenitsyn

Aleksandr Isayevich Solzhenitsyn was a Russian author, historian, soldier, and chronicler of Communist oppression during the years of the Soviet Union. When letters he wrote to a friend criticizing Joseph Stalin became known by the government, Solzhenitsyn was sentenced to eight years in labor camps and three years in Siberian exile. Despite all odds, he survived and went on to write books about his experience including The Gulag Archipelago. Solzhenitsyn was awarded the Nobel Prize for Literature in 1970 "for the ethical force with which he has pursued the traditions of Russian literature".

Born: December 11, 1918, Kislovodsk, Russia
Died: August 3, 2008, Moscow, Russia

## Stendhal

Henri-Marie Beyle, better known by his pen name Stendhal , was a 19th century French writer and soldier in the French army. He is known for his keen analysis of his characters' psychology. Stendhal was a dandy and wit about town in Paris, as well as an inveterate womaniser, which led him to contract the syphilis that eventually killed him. He was in Napoleon's doomed army that invaded Russia in 1912, but survived through clear thinking and planning. In his most famous works, Le Rouge et le Noir and La Chartreuse de Parme, he achieved great heights of Romantic Realism.

Born: January 23, 1783, Grenoble, France
Died: March 23, 1842, Paris, France

## Robert Louis Stevenson

Robert Louis Balfour Stevenson was a Scottish novelist, adventurer, travel writer, poet, and essayist. His most acclaimed works are Treasure Island, Kidnapped, and Strange Case of Dr Jekyll and Mr Hyde. He was a literary celebrity during his lifetime, and now ranks as the 26th most translated author in the world. He came from a family of lighthouse designers and engineers, but decided not to follow suit, having wanted to become a writer from an early age. His long travels, coupled with his congenital weak health, almost killed him, but his surviving use of his experiences helped bring him fame.

Born: November 13, 1850, Edinburgh, Scotland
Died: December 3, 1894, Vailima, Samoa

## Fred Smith

Frederick Wallace "Fred" Smith, is the founder, chairman, president, and CEO of FedEx, originally known as Federal Express. He is considered to be the Father of the overnight delivery business. Smith was crippled by bone disease as a small boy but regained his health by age 10, before learning to fly at 15. He had a great interest in flying, and became an amateur pilot as a teen. After graduation, Smith was commissioned in the U.S. Marine Corps, and served two tours of duty in Vietnam, flying on over 200 combat missions. He was honorably discharged in 1969 with the rank of Captain, having received the Silver Star, the Bronze Star, and two Purple Hearts.

Born: August 11, 1944

## James Stockdale

James Bond "Jim" Stockdale was a United States Navy vice admiral and aviator awarded the Medal of Honor in the Vietnam War, during which he was an American prisoner of war for over eight brutal years. He was shot down during his third tour of duty in Vietnam. By the time he was shot down, he had flown over 200 combat missions. He was the highest-ranking Navy officer to serve as a prisoner of war in Vietnam. He was awarded the Medal of Honor, which is the highest military award in the United States, as a result of his consistent leadership of the other prisoners of war that were in captivity with him.

Born: December 23, 1923, Abingdon, IL
Died: July 5, 2005, Coronado, CA

## Sun Bin

Sun Bin, who lived during the during the mid-Warring States period of Chinese history, was was considered to be one of the most outstanding Chinese military strategists after Sun Tzu. He was named Sun Bin in the ancient books because he was sentenced to a form of punishment called Bin, or branding of the face. He also had his kneecaps removed. Sun managed to escape from Wei and later rose to a prestigious role in the Qi state, by serving as a military strategist and commander. Sun wrote the military treatise Sun Bin's Art of War, which was rediscovered in 1972 during an archaeological excavation after being lost for almost 2,000 years.

Died 316 BCE, China

## Sun Tzu

Sun Tzu (birth name Sun Wu) was the author of The Art of War which is considered by many to be the best book ever written on warfare. Tzu is an honorific, meaning "master." Sun Tzu can be translated as "Master Sun." Although much of his life is unknown, he was a soldier and military strategist active during the turbulent late Chou dynasty. His string of victories brought him fame, wealth and power. Despite being praised and employed throughout East Asian warfare since its composition, The Art of War was not properly translated until the twentieth century. It presents a philosophy of war for managing conflicts and winning battles. It is accepted as a masterpiece on strategy.

Born 544 BCE, China- Died 496 BCE, China

## Herbert Swope

Herbert Bayard Swope Sr. was a U.S. editor, and journalist who became famous as a war correspondent in Germany during World War I. Once the U.S. entered the war he was commissioned as a Navy officer. Swope was the first and three-time recipient of the Pulitzer Prize for Reporting. He was called the greatest reporter of his time by Lord Northcliffe of the London Daily Mail. Born in Missouri to German immigrants, his father was a watchcase maker, but Swope achieved great financial success. He was a legendary poker player, once winning over $470,000 in a game with an oil baron and a steel magnate.

Born: January 5, 1882, St. Louis, MO
Died: June 20, 1958, Sands Point, NY

## Philip Sydney

Sir Philip Sidney was a soldier, courtier, scholar and English poet, who is remembered as one of the most notable figures of the Elizabethan age. Born into an aristocratic family, he he was elected to Parliament at the age of 18, and spent the next several years in mainland Europe, visiting France, Germany, Italy, Poland, the Kingdom of Hungary and Austria on diplomatic missions. He was knighted in 1583. He wrote the first of the famous English sonnet sequences, Astrophel and Stella, as well as An Apology for Poetry, the first supportive work of poetry criticism in the English language.

Born: November 30, 1554, Penshurst, England
Died: October 17, 1586, Zutphen, Netherlands

## Publilius Syrus

Publilius (sometimes incorrectly Publius) Syrus, was a Latin writer of maxims, who prospered in the 1st century BC. He was a Syrian who was brought to Rome as a slave, but due to his wit and talent he won the respect and admiration of his master, who freed him and educated him. His mimes, in which he acted, had a great success in the provincial towns of Italy and at the games given by Caesar in 46 BC. Publilius was perhaps even more famous as an improviser, and received from Caesar himself the prize in a contest in which he vanquished all his competitors. All that remains of his wriitings is a collection of Sententiae, a series of moral maxims in iambic and trochaic verse. He influenced Seneca the Younger, who strived to develop a "sententious style" like Publilius throughout his life.

Born c. 85 BCE
Died 43 BCE

445

## Albert Szent-Györgyi

Albert Szent-Györgyi von Nagyrápolt was a Hungarian-American physiologist who won the Nobel Prize in Physiology or Medicine in 1937 for his work in discovering Vitamin C. When Fascists took over the Hungarian government before the start of World War II, Szent-Györgyi used his influence and money to help Jewish friends escape the country. He went on to become an active member of the resistance movement working with the Allies, in hiding after Hitler ordered his arrest. After the war, he spent his life as a cancer researcher and anti-war activist.

Born: September 16, 1893, Budapest, Hungary
Died: October 22, 1986, Woods Hole, Falmouth, MA

## Tacitus

Publius (or Gaius) Cornelius Tacitus was a senator and a historian of the Roman Empire. Considered to be one of the greatest Roman historians, he lived in what has been called the Silver Age of Latin literature, and is known for the brevity and compactness of his Latin prose, as well as for his penetrating insights into the psychology of power politics. His two major works, the Annals and the Histories, examine the reigns of the emperors Tiberius, Claudius, Nero, and those who reigned in the Year of the Four Emperors (69 AD). little is known about his personal life.

Born AD 56, Roman Empire
Died AD 120, Roman Empire

## Mother Teresa

Mother Teresa was a Roman Catholic nun and missionary who spent her life taking care of the poor and disabled through the centers she built. She was born in Skopje, then part of the Kosovo Vilayet of the Ottoman Empire. In 1979 she was awarded the Nobel Peace Prize for her humanitarian work. 1950 Teresa founded the Missionaries of Charity, which manages homes for people dying of HIV/AIDS, leprosy and tuberculosis, soup kitchens, orphanages, and schools. She is remembered as one of the greatest humanitarians of the 20th century. In 2016, he was canonized as Saint Teresa of Calcutta.

Born: August 26, 1910, Skopje, Macedonia
Died: September 5, 1997, Kolkata, India

## Margaret Thatcher

Margaret Hilda Thatcher, was the first female Prime Minister of the United Kingdom (1979 to 1990). Nicknamed "The Iron Lady," she was a controversial figure in British politics. Re-elected despite bad ratings after tabloid support in the Falklands War, she used corrupt tactics to pay police to break the Miners' Strike of 1985, which ended Union effectiveness in Britain and allowed for the deregulation of society that led to the 'greed is good' culture. Her attempt to introduce an unfair 'poll tax' brought the whole country out in protest. She supported apartheid, calling Nelson Mandela a terrorist.

Born: October 13, 1925, Grantham, United Kingdom
Died: April 8, 2013, Westminster, United Kingdom

## Thucydides

Thucydides was an Athenian historian and army general. He is best known for his book The History of the Peloponnesian War which recounts the war between Sparta and Athens in the 5th Century BCE. He conducted many interviews of those involved in the war and added in his own experiences as a general during the war. Thucydides has been dubbed the father of "scientific history" by those who accept his claims to have applied strict standards of impartiality and evidence-gathering and analysis of cause and effect, without reference to intervention by the deities, as outlined in his introduction to his work.

Born: 460 BCE, Alimos, Greece
Died: 395 BCE, Athens, Greece

## Robert Townsend

Robert Chase Townsend was an American business executive and author who is noted for transforming Avis into a rental car giant. After graduating from college, he was commissioned as an officer in the United States Navy, serving for in World War II. After the war he joined American Express, rising to become senior vice president for investment and international banking. Avis was at the time a struggling auto rental company that had never made a profit in its existence. Its new owner convinced Townsend to come on board as CEO, whereupon he launched the now famous "We Try Harder" advertising campaign that turned around Avis's fortunes. His acclaimed book on business management, Up the Organization, spent 28 weeks on The New York Times Best Seller list in 1970.

Born: July 30, 1920
Died: January 12, 1998

## Harry S. Truman

Harry Truman was the 33rd U.S. president He assumed office following the death of President Franklin D. Roosevelt. In the White House from 1945 to 1953, Truman made the decision to use the atomic bomb against Japan, helped rebuild postwar Europe, worked to contain communism and led the United States into the Korean War. A Missouri native, Truman assisted in running his family farm after graduating high school and served in World War I. Three months after becoming vice president in 1945, Truman became the president. In 1948, he was reelected in an upset over Republican Thomas Dewey.

Born: May 8, 1884, Lamar, MO
Died: December 26, 1972, Kansas City, MO

## Mark Twain

Mark Twain was the pen name of Samuel Langhorne Clemens. He was an American author, satirist, publisher, entrepreneur, and lecturer. His most famous works are his novels are The Adventures of Tom Sawyer and its sequel, the Adventures of Huckleberry Finn, the latter often called "The Great American Novel". Once called the "greatest humorist this country has produced", William Faulkner called him "the father of American literature". Twain was born shortly after an appearance of Halley's Comet, and he predicted that he would "go out with it" as well; he died the day after the comet returned.

Born: November 30, 1835, Florida, MO
Died: April 21, 1910, Redding, CT

449

## Morihei Ueshiba

Morihei Ueshiba was the founder of the martial art called Aikido. He served as a soldier in the Japanese Army during the Russo-Japanese War. The name Aikido is constituted from three Japanese words: ai, meaning harmony; ki, spirit or energy; and do, the path, system or way. Ueshiba joined the Ōmoto-kyō movement, a Shinto sect, in Ayabe, where he opened his first dojo. In 1925 he had a profound spiritual experience, stating that, "a golden spirit sprang up from the ground, veiled my body, and changed my body into a golden one." After this experience, his martial arts skill appeared to be greatly increased.

Born: December 14, 1883, Tanabe, Wakayama, Japan
Died: April 26, 1969 Iwama, Ibaraki, Japan

## Brian Urquhart

Sir Brian Urquhart is a British World War II veteran, author and a former Undersecretary-General of the United Nations. When World War II broke out, Urquhart joined the Army and he and his men were part of the coastal defence forces in and around Dover during the Battle of Britain. He later transferred to the Airborne Division as an Intelligence Officer. In August 1942, he was severely injured in a training drop, damaging three vertebrae in his lower spine and breaking several bones. He spent months in the hospital recovering. In 1945, Urquhart was one of the first to enter the Bergen-Belsen concentration camp.

Born: February 28, 1919, Dorset, United Kingdom

## Vegetius

Vegetius, full name Flavius Vegetius Renatus, was a soldier and Roman military specialist who wrote what at the time was considered the single most influential military thesis in the Western world. Called De Re Militari ("Concerning Military Matters"), the book would go on to have a profound impact on how war was fought in the Middle Ages. George Washington owned a copy of this book and referred to it often. Vegetius's epitome mainly focuses on military organization and how to react to certain occasions in war. Vegetius explains how to fortify and organize a camp, how to train troops, how to handle undisciplined troops, how to handle a battle engagement, how to march, formation gauge and many other useful methods of promoting organization and valour in the legion. The work is the only ancient manual of Roman military institutions to have survived intact.

Died approx. 450 A.D.

## Lillian Vernon

Born Lilli Menasche, she was a German businesswoman and philanthropist who founded the Lillian Vernon Corporation at the age of twenty-four, with $2,000 of wedding money, by placing advertisements in Seventeen magazine for personalized purses and belts. She served as its chairwoman and CEO until July 1989. The Lillian Vernon Catalog, which the company launched in 1956, became an iconic shopping resource for American women. When the company went public in 1987, Lillian Vernon Corporation was the first company traded on the American Stock Exchange founded by a woman.

Born: March 18, 1927, Leipzig, Germany
Died: December 14, 2015 Manhattan, New York City, New York

## Leonardo da Vinci

Leonardo di ser Piero da Vinci, better known as Leonardo da Vinci, was an Italian artist, sculpture, painter, architect, inventor, scientist, intellect, military engineer, and polymath. "The Last Supper" and "Mona Lisa," are two of his most famous works. The young Leonardo received an insignificant formal education of fundamental reading, writing and mathematics instruction. His artistic talent, and insatiable curiosity were evident from a very young age. When he turned 14, da Vinci began an extended apprenticeship with the renowned artist Andrea del Verrocchio in Florence.

Born: April 15, 1452, Anchiano
Died: May 2, 1519, Clos Lucé, Amboise, France

## William Wallace

Sir William Wallace was a Scottish knight who became one of the main leaders during the Wars of Scottish Independence. Wallace led the Scottish rebellion against Edward I and inflicted a famous defeat on the English army at Stirling Bridge. He is remembered as a Scottish patriot and national hero. It's worth noting that he stood at an imposing 6' 5". Wallace was captured in Robroyston, near Glasgow, and handed over to King Edward I of England, who had him hanged, drawn, and quartered for high treason and crimes against the English. In modern times he has become an icon of independence.

Born: April 3, 1270, Elderslie, Scotland
Murdered: August 23, 1305, Smithfield, London, England

## Sam Walton

Samuel Moore "Sam" Walton was an American entrepreneur, billionaire and businessman who founded the stores Walmart and Sam's Club. Walton opened his first retail store at the age of 27 after he had saved $5,000 and borrowed $20,000 from his father-in-law. Wal-Mart grew to be the world's largest corporation by revenue as well as the biggest private employer in the world. At one point in his life, he was the richest man in America. In1998 Walton was included in Time's list of 100 most influential people of the 20th Century. He received the Presidential Medal of Freedom from President George H. W. Bush.

Born: March 29, 1918, Kingfisher, OK
Died: April 5, 1992, Little Rock, AR

## William Arthur Ward

William Arthur Ward was a former U.S. Army Captain who became a motivational speaker and author. More than 100 articles, poems and meditations written by Ward wre published in such magazines as Reader's Digest, The Phi Delta Kappan, and Science of Mind. His column "Pertinent Proverbs" was published by the Fort Worth Star-Telegram and also in American service club publications. He was a frequently quoted writer in Quote, an international weekly digest for public speakers. A graduate of McMurry College, he received his master's degree at Oklahoma State University. In 1962 he was awarded an honorary Oklahoma City University degree in recognition of his "professional achievement, literary contributions and service to others."

Born in Louisiana 1921
Died: March 30, 1994

## George Washington

Washington was the first president of the United States of America, and commander of the Continental Army during America's war for independence against the British. Born to a successful family of planters and slaveholders in colonial Virginia, he became a leader of the Virginia militia in the French and Indian War. During the Revolutionary War he was a delegate to the Continental Congress, and was unanimously appointed commander-in-chief of the Army. Washington was a lifelong student, and a voracious reader. He had over 900 books in his library when he died.

Born: February 22, 1732, Westmoreland County, Virginia, VA
Died: December 14, 1799, Mount Vernon, VA

## Thomas J. Watson Jr.

Watson was an American business executive, and philanthropist. He was the 2nd president of IBM (1952–1971). Watson was the CEO during IBM's meteoric period of growth from a gross revenue of $892 million in 1956 to $8.3 billion when he stepped down in 1971. He is credited with taking IBM into the computer age. During World War II, Watson served five years as a pilot in the U.S. Army Air Corps. He was awarded the Presidential Medal of Freedom by Lyndon B. Johnson and was the 16th United States Ambassador to the Soviet Union (1979–1981).

Born: January 14, 1914, Dayton, OH
Died: December 31, 1993, Greenwich, CT

## Jeff Weiner

Jeff Weiner is the CEO of LinkedIn. In 2016, when LinkedIn's stock price plunged 40%, Weiner donated his $14 million stock bonus to employees to make up for the drop. Weiner played an instrumental role in LinkedIn's acquisition by Microsoft for $26 billion in June 2016. Graduated from The Wharton School at the University of Pennsylvania in 1992 with a Bachelor of Science in Economics, Weiner served in various leadership roles at Yahoo for over seven years beginning in 2001, most recently as the Executive Vice President of Yahoo's Network Division. He has worked at Warner Bros. as Vice President of Warner Bros. Online, developing its initial business plan.

Born: February 21, 1970, New York City, NY

## Jack Welch

John Francis Welch, Jr., mainly known as Jack Welch in the business world, was the chairman and CEO of General Electric. He led the company to double-digit growth during his two decades as CEO. As the new CEO, Welch launched a strategy that earned him the nickname "Neutron Jack." He had GE cut all businesses in which the company could not dominate the market in either the first or second positions. He then had managers fire the bottom 10 percent of GE employees, while he fired the bottom 10 percent of management. Welch's housecleaning swept away layers of calcified bureaucracy that had built up at the company and made way for a rapid stream of ideas.

Born: November 19, 1935, Peabody, MA

## Arthur Wellesley, Duke of Wellington

The First Duke of Wellington, Arthur Wellesley (The Iron Duke) was an Anglo-Irish soldier and statesman, and one of the leading military and political figures of 19th-century Britain. Mostly remembered for his victory over Napoleon at the Battle of Waterloo (1815), he served twice as Prime Minister. He spent his formative military years in India, where he fought in the Fourth Anglo-Mysore War at the Battle of Seringapatam and, as a newly appointed major-general, won a decisive victory over the Maratha Confederacy at the Battle of Assaye in 1803.

Born: May 1, 1769, Dublin, Ireland
Died: September 14, 1852, Walmer Castle, England

## William H. Whyte

William Hollingsworth "Holly" Whyte was an author, journalist and student of human nature in the modern environment. Whyte graduated from Princeton University and served in the Marine Corps during World War. He went on to write for Fortune magazine, and wrote the book The Organization Man, which was based on his articles about the dysfunction of corporate culture and the suburban middle class. The book would go on to sell over two million copies. Whyte coined the term "Groupthink", "a philosophy which holds that group values are not only expedient but right and good as well".

Born: October 1, 1917, West Chester, PA
Died: January 12, 1999, New York City, NY

## John "Jocko" Willink

John "Jocko" Willink is a legendary retired United States Navy SEAL, who received the Silver Star and Bronze Star for his actions in the Iraq War. Willink was commander of SEAL Team Three's Task Unit Bruiser during the 2006 Battle of Ramadi, which is considered some of the most severe and most continuous combat by the SEAL Teams since Vietnam. Task Unit Bruiser was the most highly decorated special operations unit of the Iraq War. He went on to co-found the consulting firm Echelon Front. Willink hosts a weekly podcast with friend and Brazilian jiu jitsu practitioner Echo Charles, called 'The Jocko Podcast'.

Born Torrington, Connecticut September 8, 1971

## Dr. Charles McMoran Wilson

Dr. Charles McMoran Wilson is most well known for being Sir Winston Churchill's personal physician. The son of a phyician who trained at the Imperial College School of Medicine, he served with valor as a medic during the horrific trench warfare of World War I. He was medical officer to the 1st Battalion of the Royal Fusiliers from 1914 to 1917 and medical officer in charge of the medical facilities at the British 7th Stationary Hospital in Boulogne from 1917 to 1918. He won the Military Cross in 1916 for services during the Battle of the Somme, and the Italian Silver Medal of Military Valour in 1917.

Born: November 10, 1882, Skipton, United Kingdom
Died: April 12, 1977, Hampshire, United Kingdom

## Robert Anton Wilson

Wilson was an American author, futurist, libertarian, editor, essayist, philosopher, polymath, and psychonaut. He characterized his work as an "attempt to break down conditioned associations, to look at the world in a new way, with many models recognized as models or maps, and no one model elevated to the truth." He once wrote, ""Is", "is." "is"—the idiocy of the word haunts me. If it were abolished, human thought might begin to make sense. I don't know what anything "is"; I only know how it seems to me at this moment." He wrote 35 books and many other works, including plays and screenplays.

Born: January 18, 1932, Brooklyn, New York City, NY
Died: January 11, 2007, Capitola, CA

## John Wooden

Wooden was the first person to be inducted into the Basketball Hall of Fame both as a player and coach. Nicknamed the "Wizard of Westwood," as head coach at UCLA he won ten NCAA national championships in a 12-year period, including a record seven in a row. ESPN ranks him as the greatest coach of all time across all sports. In his 40 years at UCLA, he mentored legends such as Bill Walton and Kareem Abdul-Jabbar. Wooden wanted his players to be champions in life as well as the court, so he treated them as family and stressed that winning wasn't just about scoring on the court.

Born: October 14, 1910, Hall, IN
Died: June 4, 2010, Los Angeles, CA

## William Wrigley Jr.

William Wrigley Jr. was the founder of William Wrigley Jr. and Company of chewing gum fame. Wrigley formed a business to sell Wrigley's Scouring Soap. He offered customers baking powder as an incentive to buy his soap. Finding the baking powder was more popular than his soap, Wrigley switched to selling baking powder, giving his customers chewing gum for each can of baking powder they purchased. Again, Wrigley found that the premium he offered was more popular than his base product, and his company began to concentrate on the manufacture and sale of chewing gum, making his fortune.

Born: September 30, 1861, Philadelphia, PA
Died: January 26, 1932, Phoenix, AZ)

## Wu Qi

Wu Qi was a Chinese military leader, legalist philosopher, and politician in the Warring States period. Wu's reforms, which started around 389 BC, were aimed at changing the corrupt and inefficient government. Another of Wu's actions was to move all the nobles to the borders on the frontier. According to the Wei Liaozi, a treatise on military matters dating from the late 4th or early 3rd century BC, the general Wu Qi was once offered a sword by his subordinates on the eve of battle. However Wu Qi refused to accept the weapon on the basis that banners and drums, the tools to lead and command, were the only instruments a general required. The reforms he instituted enraged the old nobility of Chu and he was killed after the death of his patron King Dao.

Born: 440 CE, China
Died: 381 BCE, China

## Xenophon

Xenophon of Athens was an ancient Greek philosopher, historian, soldier and mercenary, a contemporary of Plato and a student of Socrates. He was considered a man of words and a man of action. As a soldier, Xenophon became commander of the Ten Thousand at about 29, with one military historian saying of him, "the centuries since have devised nothing to surpass the genius of this warrior." As a historian, Xenophon is known for recording the history of his time, the late 5th and early 4th centuries BC in such works as the Hellenica, which covered the final seven years and the aftermath of the Peloponnesian War.

Born: 431 BCE, Erchia
Died: 354 BCE, Thrace

## Tsunetomo Yamamoto

Tsunetomo Yamamoto was a samurai of the Saga Domain who devoted his life to the service of his lord and clan. After his master's death Yamamoto renounced the world and retired to a hermitage in the mountains. Later in life he narrated many of his thoughts to a fellow samurai, Tashiro Tsuramoto. Many of these aphorisms concerned his lord's father and grandfather Naoshige and the failing ways of the samurai caste. These commentaries were compiled and published in 1716 under the title of Hagakure, a word that can be translated as either In the Shadow of Leaves or Hidden Leaves.

Born: June 11, 1659
Died: November 30, 1719

## John Zenger

John Peter Zenger was a German American printer and journalist in New York City. Zenger printed The New York Weekly Journal. Zengar immigrated to New York City at 13, and was indentured for eight years as an apprentice. By 1726 he had founded his own printing business. He is best known for being accused of libel by the governor of New York. This was one of the first major court cases regarding the freedom of speech and the press. Zengar was acquitted after a long jury trial. His lawyers successfully argued that truth is a defense against charges of libel.

Born: October 26, 1697, Impflingen, Germany
Died: July 28, 1746, New York City, NY

## Zhang Liang

Zhang Liang was a chief military strategist and minister. He is credited with creating the book, The Three Strategies of Huang Shigong, which is a book on military strategy. It is one of China's Seven Military Classics. Zhang Liang was famous for his ability to "win battles 1,000 miles away without stepping outside the command tent." Along with his tremendous flair for creating unique military strategies, he was also admired and respected for his reverence for the elderly, and for his humble and prudent way of life. He is known as one of the "Three Heroes of the early Han dynasty".

Born c. 262 BCE, China
Died 189 BCE, China

# Epilogue

"Be ashamed to die until you have won some victory for humanity."
— Horace Mann

Horace Mann was an American education reformer, politician, and the first great advocate of public education in order to preserve the republic. Despite growing up in poverty, and being mostly self-educated, he went on to help create a universal education system. (Born May 4, 1796, Franklin, Mass., U.S. Died Aug. 2, 1859, Yellow Springs, Ohio)

"I remember clearly the deaths of three men. One was the richest man of the century, who, having clawed his way to wealth through the souls and bodies of men, spent many years trying to buy back the love he had forfeited and by that process performed great service to the world and, perhaps, had much more than balanced the evils of his rise. I was on a ship when he died. The news was posted on the bulletin board, and nearly everyone received the news with pleasure. Several said, "Thank God that son of a bitch is dead."

Then there was a man, smart as Satan, who, lacking some perception of human dignity and knowing all too well every aspect of human weakness and wickedness, used his special knowledge to warp men, to buy men, to bribe and threaten and seduce until he found himself in a position of great power. He clothed his motives in the names of virtue, and I have wondered whether he ever knew that no gift will ever buy back a man's love when you have removed his self-love. A bribed man can only hate his briber. When this man died the nation rang with praise...

There was a third man, who perhaps made many errors in

performance but whose effective life was devoted to making men brave and dignified and good in a time when they were poor and frightened and when ugly forces were loose in the world to utilize their fears. This man was hated by few. When he died the people burst into tears in the streets and their minds wailed, "What can we do now? How can we go on without him?"

In uncertainty I am certain that underneath their topmost layers of frailty men want to be good and want to be loved. Indeed, most of their vices are attempted short cuts to love. When a man comes to die, no matter what his talents and influence and genius, if he dies unloved his life must be a failure to him and his dying a cold horror... we should remember our dying and try so to live that our death brings no pleasure to the world."

– John Steinbeck, East of Eden

"Look again at that dot. That's here. That's home. That's us. On it everyone you love, everyone you know, everyone you ever heard of, every human being who ever was, lived out their lives. The aggregate of our joy and suffering, thousands of confident religions, ideologies, and economic doctrines, every hunter and forager, every hero and coward, every creator and destroyer of civilization, every king and peasant, every young couple in love, every mother and father, hopeful child, inventor and explorer, every teacher of morals, every corrupt politician, every "superstar," every "supreme leader," every saint and sinner in the history of our species lived there — on a mote of dust suspended in a sunbeam.

The Earth is a very small stage in a vast cosmic arena. Think of the endless cruelties visited by the inhabitants of one corner of this pixel on the scarcely distinguishable inhabitants of some other corner, how frequent their misunderstandings, how eager they are to kill one another, how fervent their hatreds. Think of the rivers of blood spilled by all those generals and emperors so that, in glory and triumph, they could become the momentary masters of a fraction of a dot.

Our posturings, our imagined self-importance, the delusion that we have some privileged position in the Universe, are challenged by this point of pale light. Our planet is a lonely speck in the great enveloping cosmic dark. In our obscurity, in all this vastness, there is no hint that help will come from elsewhere to save us from ourselves.

The Earth is the only world known so far to harbor life. There is nowhere else, at least in the near future, to which our species could migrate. Visit, yes. Settle, not yet. Like it or not, for the moment the Earth is where we make our stand.

It has been said that astronomy is a humbling and character-building experience. There is perhaps no better demonstration of the folly of human conceits than this distant image of our tiny world. To me, it underscores our responsibility to deal more kindly with one another, and to preserve and cherish the pale blue dot, the only home we've ever known."

– Carl Sagan (Pale Blue Dot: A Vision of the Human Future in Space)

I hope you have enjoyed this guide and that it continues to serve you for a lifetime.

Feel free to write me at Derek@TheWisdomOfLeaders.com

# About the Editor

Derek Wellington Johnson's background brings a unique perspective to the study of great leadership. He is a military veteran, a startup veteran and a lifelong student of human nature and history.

With two decades of sales leadership experience in the high tech world, Derek is recognized as a technology expert and a trusted advisor to C-level decision makers. His expertise has led to him being repeatedly quoted in publications such as Inc. Magazine, Investor's Business Daily, Network World Magazine, CNet News, CIO Magazine, and PC World, to name a few. He has appeared on radio and television.

Derek was an original member of the board of directors on the Fiber to the Home (FTTH) Council, (now called the Fiber Broadband Association) a consortium of companies dedicated to bringing Broadband Internet to Americans everywhere. The current ubiquity of Broadband today is proof of the organization's success.

He is currently in a leadership position for a high tech company and may be reached for speaking engagements at Derek@ TheWisdomOfLeaders.com

# Index by full name

# Index by last names

Made in the USA
Columbia, SC
17 March 2019